THE CHARLES G. FINNEY
MEMORIAL LIBRARY

VICTORY

over the

WORLD

VICTORY
over the
WORLD

Revival Messages

CHARLES G. FINNEY

KREGEL PUBLICATIONS
GRAND RAPIDS, MICHIGAN 49501

Library of Congress Catalog Card Number 66-24879
ISBN 0-8254-2619-7

This series of sermons selected from
LECTURES TO PROFESSING CHRISTIANS and GOSPEL THEMES
by Charles G. Finney

Reprinted 1975

Printed in the United States of America

PUBLISHER'S FOREWORD

Why this new edition of the sermons of Charles Grandison Finney? Because in many ways the days in which we are living are a duplicate of the day and situation in which Finney himself proclaimed the message which God had given him — the call to evangelism and to revival. These messages speak to our day in no uncertain sound for conditions within the church, and in the world around, call for a voice from God, a resounding clarion call for return to the Biblical standard of Christian life, and the God-ordained plan of redemption and revival.

These have been chosen and arranged with the needs of the world and church today in view. They are as applicable in this day of falling away and departure from the faith as they were in Finney's day. Heart-searching and uncompromising, they cut away the froth and frills so apparent in much modern preaching to reveal God's message for a sinning world, a world seemingly intent upon self-destruction and self-aggrandizement.

It is the publisher's prayer that these messages in their new form will convey God's message to our needy world, revealing His will and purpose for His Church — and His divine plan of salvation for an unbelieving generation.

The Publishers

CONTENTS

1

VICTORY OVER THE WORLD

"For whatsoever is born of God overcometh the world: and this is the victory that overcometh the world, even our faith." —I John 5:4.

THE discussion of this text naturally leads us to make four inquiries:

I. What is it to overcome the world?

II. Who are they that overcome?

III. Why do they overcome the world?

IV. How do they do it?

These are the natural questions which a serious mind would ask upon reading this text.

I. *What is it to overcome the world?*

1. It is to get above the spirit of covetousness which possesses the men of the world. The spirit of the world is eminently the spirit of covetousness. It is a greediness after the things of the world. Some worldly men covet one thing and some another; but all classes of worldly men are living in the spirit of covetousness in some of its forms. This spirit has supreme possession of their minds.

Now the first thing in overcoming the world is, that the spirit of covetousness in respect to worldly things and objects be overcome. The man who does not overcome this spirit of bustling and scrambling after the good which this world proffers has by no means overcome it.

2. Overcoming the world implies rising above its engross-

ments. When a man has overcome the world his thoughts are no longer engrossed and swallowed up with worldly things. A man certainly does not overcome the world unless he gets above being engrossed and absorbed with its concerns.

Now we all know how exceedingly engrossed worldly men are with some form of worldly good. One is swallowed up with study; another with politics; a third with money-getting; and a fourth perhaps with fashion and with pleasure; but each in his chosen way makes earthly good the all-engrossing object.

The man who gains the victory over the world must overcome not one form only of its pursuits, but every form—must overcome the world itself and all that it has to present as an allurement to the human heart.

3. Overcoming the world implies overcoming the fear of the world.

It is a mournful fact that most men, and indeed all men of worldly character, have so much regard to public opinion that they dare not act according to the dictates of their consciences when acting thus would incur the popular frown. One is afraid lest his business should suffer if his course runs counter to public opinion; another fears lest if he stand up for the truth it will injure his reputation, and curiously imagines and tries to believe that advocating an unpopular truth will diminish and perhaps destroy his good influence—as if a man could exert a good influence in any possible way besides maintaining the *truth*.

Great multitudes, it must be admitted, are under this influence of fearing the world; yet some, perhaps many, of them, are not aware of this fact. If you or if they could thoroughly sound the reasons of their backwardness in duty, fear of the world would be found among the chief. Their fear of the world's displeasure is so much stronger than their fear of God's displeasure that they are completely enslaved by it. Who does not know that some ministers dare not preach what they know is true, and even what they know is *important* truth, lest they should offend some whose good opinion they seek to retain ? The society is weak, perhaps, and the favour of some rich man in it seems indispensable to its very existence. Hence the terror of these rich men is continually before their eyes when they write a sermon, or preach, or are called to take a stand in favour of any truth or cause which may be unpopular with men of more wealth than piety or conscience. Alas! this bondage to man! Too many Gospel ministers are so troubled by it that their time-serving policy is virtually renouncing Christ and serving the world.

Overcoming the world is thoroughly subduing this servility to men.

4. Overcoming the world implies overcoming a state of *worldly anxiety*. You know there is a state of great careful-ness and anxiety which is common and almost universal among worldly men. It is perfectly natural if the heart is set upon securing worldly good, and has not learned to receive all good from the hand of a great Father and trust Him to give or withhold with His own unerring wisdom. But he who loves the world is the enemy of God, and hence can never have this filial trust in a parental Benefactor, nor the peace of soul which it imparts. Hence worldly men are almost incessantly in a fever of anxiety lest their worldly schemes should fail. They sometimes get a momentary relief when all things seem to go well ; but some mishap is sure to befall them at some point soon, so that scarce a day passes that brings not with it some corroding anxiety. Their bosoms are like the troubled sea which cannot rest, whose waters cast up mire and dirt.

But the man who gets above the world gets above this state of ceaseless and corroding anxiety.

5. The victory under consideration implies that we cease

to be enslaved and in bondage to the world in any of its forms.

There is a worldly spirit and there is also a heavenly spirit ; and one or the other exists in the heart of every man and controls his whole being.   Those who are under the control of the world, of course have not overcome the world.   No man overcomes the world till his heart is imbued with the spirit of heaven.

One form which the spirit of the world assumes is—being enslaved to the customs and fashions of the day.

It is marvellous to see what a goddess Fashion becomes.   No heathen goddess was ever worshipped with costlier offerings or more devout homage or more implicit subjection.   And surely no heathen deity since the world began has ever had more universal patronage.   Where will you go to find the man of the world or the woman of the world who does not hasten to worship at her shrine ?

But overcoming the world implies that the spell of this goddess is broken.

They who have overcome the world are no longer careful either to secure its favour or avert its frown ; and the good or the ill opinion of the world is to them a small matter.   " To me," said Paul, " it is a small thing to be judged of man's judgment."   So of every real Christian ; his care is to secure the approbation of God ; this is his chief concern, to commend himself to God and to his own conscience.   No man has overcome the world unless he has attained this state of mind.

Almost no feature of Christian character is more striking or more decisive than this—*indifference to the opinions of the world*.

Since I have been in the ministry I have been blessed with the acquaintance of some men who were peculiarly distinguished by this quality of character.   Some of you may have known Rev. James Patterson, late of Philadelphia.   If so, you know him to have been eminently distinguished in this respect. He seemed to have the least possible disposition to secure the applause of men or avoid their censure. It seemed to be of no consequence to him to commend himself to men. For him it was enough if he might please God.

Hence you were sure to find him in everlasting war against sin, all sin, however popular, however entrenched by custom or sustained by wealth, or public opinion. Yet he always opposed sin with a most remarkable spirit—a spirit of inflexible decision and yet of great mellowness and tenderness. While he was saying the most severe things in the most decided language, you might see the big tears rolling down his cheeks.

It is wonderful that most men never complained of his having a bad spirit. Much as they dreaded his rebuke and writhed under his strong and daring exposures of wickedness, they could never say that Father Patterson had any other than a good spirit. This was a most beautiful and striking exemplification of having overcome the world.

Men who are not thus dead to the world have not escaped its bondage. The victorious Christian is in a state where he is no longer in bondage to man. He is *bound* only to serve God.

II. We must inquire, *Who are those that overcome the world?*

Our text gives the ready answer : "Whatsoever is born of God overcometh the world." You cannot fail to observe that this is a universal proposition—all who are born of God overcome the world—all these, and it is obviously implied none others. You may know who are born of God by this characteristic—they overcome the world. Of course the second question is answered.

III. Our next question is, why do believers overcome the world? *On what principle is this result effected?*

I answer, this victory over the world results as naturally from the spiritual or heavenly birth, as coming into bondage to the world results from the natural birth.

It may be well to revert a moment to the law of connection in the latter case, viz., between coming into the world by natural birth and bondage to the world. This law obviously admits of a philosophical explanation, at once simple and palpable to every one's observation. Natural birth reveals to the mind objects of sense and these only. It brings the mind into contact with worldly things. Of course it is natural that the mind should become deeply interested in these objects thus presented through its external senses, especially as most of them sustain so intimate a relation to our sentient nature and become the first and chief sources of our happiness.

Hence our affections are gradually entwined around these objects, and we become thoroughly lovers of this world ere our eyes have been opened upon it many months.

Now alongside of this universal fact let another be placed of equal importance and not less universal, namely, that those intuitive powers of the mind which were created to take cognizance of our moral relations, and hence to counteract the too great influence of worldly objects, come into action very slowly, and are not developed so as to act vigorously until years are numbered as months are in the case of the external organs of sense. The very early and vigorous development of the latter brings the soul so entirely under the control of worldly objects that when the reason and the conscience come to speak, their voice is little heeded. As a matter of fact, we find it universally true that unless divine power interpose, the bondage to the world thus induced upon the soul is never broken.

But the point which I particularly desired to elucidate was simply this, that natural birth, with its attendant laws of physical and mental development, becomes the occasion of bondage to this world.

Right over against this lies the birth into the kingdom of God by the Spirit. By this the soul is brought into new relations—we might rather say, into intimate contact with spiritual things. The Spirit of God seems to usher the soul into the spiritual world, in a manner strictly analogous to the result of the natural birth upon our physical being. The great truths of the spiritual world are opened to our view through the illumination of the Spirit of God ; we seem to see with new eyes, and to have a new world of spiritual objects around us.

As in regard to natural objects, men not only speculate about them, but *realize* them ; so in the case of spiritual children do spiritual things become not merely matters of speculation, but of full and practical *realization* also. When God reveals Himself to the mind, spiritual things are seen in their real light, and make the impression of realities.

Consequently, when spiritual objects are thus revealed to the mind, and thus apprehended, they will supremely interest that mind. Such is our mental constitution that the truth of God when thoroughly apprehended cannot fail to interest us. If these truths were clearly revealed to the wickedest man on earth, so that he should apprehend them as realities, it could not fail to rouse up his soul to most intense action. He might hate the light, and might stubbornly resist the claims of God upon his heart, but he could not fail to feel a thrilling interest in truths that so take hold of the great and vital things of human well-being.

Let me ask, is there a sinner in this house, or can there be a sinner on this wide earth, who does not see that if God's presence was made as manifest and as real to his mind as the presence of his fellow-men, it would supremely engross his soul even though it might not subdue his heart.

This revelation of God's presence and character might not convert him, but it would, at least for the time being, kill his attention to the world.

You often see this in the case of persons deeply convicted ; you have doubtless seen persons so fearfully convicted of sin, that they cared nothing at all for their food nor their dress. O, they cried out in the agony of their souls, what matter all these things to us, if we even get them all, and then must lie down in hell !

But these thrilling and all-absorbing convictions do not necessarily convert the soul, and I have alluded to them here only to show the controlling power of realizing views of divine truth.

When real conversion has taken place, and the soul is born of God, then realizing views of truth not only awaken interest, as they might do in an unrenewed mind, but they also tend to excite a deep and ardent love for these truths. They draw out the heart. Spiritual truth now takes possession of his mind, and draws him into its warm and life-giving embrace. Before, error, falsehood, death, had drawn him under their power ; now the Spirit of God draws him into the very embrace of God. Now he is begotten of God, and breathes the spirit of sonship. Now, according to the Bible, "the seed of God remaineth in him," that very truth, and those movings of the spirit which give him birth into the kingdom of God, continue still in power upon his mind, and hence he continues a Christian, and as the Bible states it, "he cannot sin, because he is born of God." The seed of God is in him, and the fruit of it brings his soul deeply into sympathy with his own Father in heaven.

Again, the first birth makes us acquainted with earthly things, the second with God ; the first with the finite, the second with the infinite ; the first with things correlated with our animal nature, the second with those great things which stand connected with our spiritual nature, things so lovely, and so glorious as to overcome all the ensnarements of the world.

Again, the first begets a worldly, and the second a heavenly temper. Under the first, the mind is brought into a snare , under the second, it is delivered from that snare. Under the first, the conversation is earthly ; under the second, " our conversation is in heaven."

But we must pass to inquire,—

IV. *How this victory over the world is achieved.*

The great agent is the Holy Spirit. Without Him, no good result is ever achieved in the Christian's heart or life.

The text, you observe, says, " This is the victory that overcometh the world, even our faith." But here the question might be raised : Does this mean that faith of itself overcomes the world, or, is this the meaning, that we overcome by or through our faith ? Doubtless the latter is the precise meaning. Believing in God, and having realizing impressions of His truth and character made upon our mind by the Holy Ghost given to those who truly believe, we gain the victory over the world.

Faith implies three things. 1. Perception of truth. 2. An interest in it. 3. The committal or giving up of the mind to be interested and controlled by these objects of faith.

Perception of the truth must come first in order, for there can be no belief of unknown and unperceived truth. Next, there must be an interest in the truth which shall wake up the mind to fixed and active attention ; and thirdly, there must be a voluntary committal of the mind to the control of truth. The mind must wholly yield itself up to God, to be governed entirely by His will, and to trust Him and Him alone as its own present and eternal portion.

Again, faith receives Christ. The mind first perceives Christ's character and His relations to us—sees what He does for us, and then deeply feeling its own need of such a Saviour, and of such a work wrought in and for us as Jesus alone can do, it goes forth to receive and embrace Jesus as its own Saviour. This action of the soul in receiving and embracing Christ is not sluggish—it is not a state of dozing quietism. No ; it involves the soul's most strenuous activity. And this committal of the soul must become a glorious, living, energizing principle—the mind not only perceiving, but yielding itself up with the most fervid intensity to be Christ's and to receive all the benefits of His salvation into our own souls.

Again, faith receives Christ into the soul as King, in all His relations, to rule over the whole being—to have our heart's supreme confidence and affection—to receive the entire homage of our obedience and adoration ; to rule, in short, over us, and fulfil all the functions of supreme King over our whole moral being. Within our very souls we receive Christ to live and energize there, to reign forever there as on His own rightful throne.

Now a great many seem to stop short of this entire and perfect committal of their whole soul to Christ. They stop short perhaps with merely *perceiving* the truth, satisfied and pleased that they have learned the theory of the Gospel. Or perhaps some go one step further, and stop with being interested—with having their feelings excited by the things of the Gospel, thus going only to the second stage ; or perhaps they seem to take faith, but not Christ; they think to believe, but after all do not cordially and with all the heart welcome Christ Himself into the soul.

All these various steps stop short of really taking hold of Christ. They none of them result in giving the victory over the world.

The true Bible doctrine of faith represents Christ as coming into the very soul. "Behold I stand at the door and knock ; if any man hear My voice and open the door, I will come in to him and sup with him, and he with Me." What could more forcibly and beautifully teach the doctrine that by faith Christ is introduced into the very soul of the believer to dwell there by His gracious presence ?

Since my mind has been drawn to the subject, I have

been astonished to see how long I have been in a purblind state of perception in respect to this particular view of faith. Of a long time I had scarcely seen it ; now I see it beaming forth in lines of glory on almost every page. The Bible seems to blaze with the glorious truth, Christ *in the soul,* the hope of glory ; God, Christ, dwelling in our body as in a temple. I am amazed that a truth so rich and so blessed should have been seen so dimly, when the Bible reveals it so plainly. Christ received into the very soul by faith, and thus brought into the nearest possible relations to our heart and life ; Christ Himself becoming the all-sustaining Power within us, and thus securing the victory over the world ; Christ, living and energizing in our hearts—this is the great central truth in the plan of sanctification, and this no Christian should fail to understand, as he values the victory over the world and the living communion of the soul with its Maker.

CONCLUSION

1. It is in the very nature of the case impossible that if faith receive Christ into the soul, it should not overcome the world. If the new birth actually brings the mind into this new state, and brings Christ into the soul, then, of course, Christ will reign in that soul ; the supreme affections will be yielded most delightfully to Him, and the power of the world over that mind will be broken. Christ cannot dwell in any soul without absorbing the supreme interest of that soul. And this is, of course, equivalent to giving the victory over the world.

2. He who does not habitually overcome the world is not born of God. In saying this, I do not intend to affirm that a true Christian may not sometimes be overcome by sin ; but I do affirm that overcoming the world is the general rule, and falling into sin is only the exception. This is the least that can be meant by the language of our text and by similar

declarations which often occur in the Bible. Just as in the passage—" He that is born of God doth not commit sin, and he cannot sin because he is born of God," nothing less can be meant than this—that he cannot sin uniformly ; cannot make sinning his business, and can sin, if at all, only occasionally and aside from the general current of his life. In the same manner we should say of a man who is in general truthful, that he is not a liar.

I will not contend for more than this respecting either of these passages ; but for so much as this I must contend, that the new-born souls here spoken of *do in general overcome* the world. The general fact respecting them is that they do not sin and are not in bondage to Satan. The affirmations of Scripture respecting them must at least embrace their general character.

3. What is a religion good for that does not overcome the world ? What is the benefit of being born into such a religion if it leave the world still swaying its dominion over our hearts ? What avails a new birth which after all fails to bring us into a likeness to God, into the sympathies of His family and of His kingdom ; which leaves us still in bondage to the world and to Satan ? What can there be of such a religion more than the name ? With what reason can any man suppose that such a religion fits his heart for heaven, supposing it leaves him earthly-minded, sensual, and selfish.

4. We see why it is that infidels have proclaimed the Gospel of Christ to be a failure. You may not be aware that of late infidels have taken the ground that the Gospel of Christ is a failure. They maintain that it professes to bring men out from the world, but fails to do so ; and hence is manifestly a failure. Now you must observe that the Bible does indeed affirm, as infidels say, that those who are truly born of God do overcome the world. This we cannot deny, and should not wish to deny it. Now, if the infidel can show that the new birth fails to produce this result, he has

carried his point, and we must yield ours. This is perfectly plain, and there can be no escape for us.

But the infidel is in fault in his premises. He assumes the current Christianity of the age as a specimen of real religion, and builds his estimate upon this. He proves, as he thinks, and perhaps proves truly, that the current Christianity does not overcome the world.

We must demur to his assuming this current Christianity as real religion. For this religion of the mass of nominal professors does not answer the descriptions given of true piety in the Word of God. And, moreover, if this current type of religion were all that the Gospel and the Divine Spirit can do for lost man, then we might as well give up the point in controversy with the infidel; for such a religion could not give us much evidence of coming from God, and would be of very little value to man; so little as scarcely to be worth contending for. Truly, if we must take the professedly Christian world as Bible Christians, who would not be ashamed and confounded in attempting to confront the infidel? We know but too well that the great mass of professed Christians do not overcome the world, and we should be confounded quickly if we were to maintain that they do. Those professed Christians themselves know that they do not overcome the world. Of course they could not testify concerning themselves that in their own case the power of the Gospel is exemplified.

In view of facts like these, I have often been astonished to see ministers setting themselves to persuade their people that they are really converted, trying to lull their fears and sustain their tottering hopes. Vain effort! Those same ministers, it would seem, must know that they themselves do not overcome the world; and equally well must they know that their people do not. How fatal, then, to the soul must be such efforts to "heal the hurt of God's professed people slightly; crying, Peace, peace, when there is no peace!"

Let us sift this matter to the bottom, pushing the inquiry—
Do the great mass of professed Christians really overcome the
world? It is a fact beyond question that with them the
things of this world are the realities, and the things of God
are mere theories. Who does not know that this is the real
state of great multitudes in the nominal Church?

Let the searching inquiry run through this congregation—
What are those things that set your soul on fire—that stir up
your warmest emotions and deeply agitate your nervous
system? Are these the things of earth, or the things of
heaven? the things of time, or the things of eternity? the
things of self, or the things of God?

How is it when you go into your closets? Do you go there
to seek and find God? Do you in fact find there a present
God, and do you hold communion there as friend with friend?
How is this?

Now you certainly should know that if your state is such
that spiritual things are mere theories and speculations, you
are altogether worldly and nothing more. It would be egre-
gious folly and falsehood to call you spiritual-minded, and
for you to think yourselves spiritual would be the most fatal
and foolish self-deception. You give none of the appropriate
proofs of being born of God. Your state is not that of one
who is personally acquainted with God, and who loves Him
personally with supreme affection.

5. Until we can put away from the minds of men the common error that the current Christianity of the Church
is true Christianity, we can make but little progress in
converting the world. For in the first place, we cannot
save the Church itself from bondage to the world in this
life, nor from the direst doom of the hypocrite in the
next. We cannot unite and arm the Church in vigorous
onset upon Satan's kingdom, so that the world may be converted to God. We cannot even convince intelligent men
of the world that our religion is from God, and brings to

fallen men a remedy for their depravity. For if the common Christianity of the age is the best that can be, and this does not give men the victory over the world, what is it good for? And if it really is of little worth or none, how can we hope to make thinking men prize it as of great value?

6. There are but very few infidels who are as much in the dark as they profess to be on these points. There are very few of that class of men who are not acquainted with some humble Christians, whose lives commend Christianity and condemn their own ungodliness. Of course they know the truth, that there is a reality in the religion of the Bible, and they blind their own eyes selfishly and most foolishly when they try to believe that the religion of the Bible is a failure, and that the Bible is therefore a fabrication. Deep in their heart lies the conviction that here and there are men who are real Christians, who overcome the world and live by a faith unknown to themselves. In how many cases does God set some burning examples of Christian life before those wicked, sceptical men, to rebuke them for their sin and their scepticism—perhaps their own wife or their children, their neighbours or their servants. By such means the truth is lodged in their mind, and God has a witness for Himself in their consciences.

I have perhaps before mentioned a fact which occurred at the South, and was stated to me by a minister of the Gospel who was acquainted with the circumstances of the case. There resided in that region a very worldly and a most ungodly man, who held a great slave property, and was withal much given to horse-racing. Heedless of all religion and avowedly sceptical, he gave full swing to every evil propensity. But wicked men must one day see trouble; and this man was taken sick and brought to the very gates of the grave. His weeping wife and friends gather round his bed, and begin to think of having some Christian called in to pray for the dying man's soul. Husband, said the anxious wife, shall I not send for our minister to pray with you before you die ? No, said he, I know him of old ; I have no confidence in him ; I have seen him too many times at horse-races ; there he was my friend and I was his ; but I don't want to see him now.

But who shall we get, then ? continued the wife. Send for my slave Tom, replied he ; he is one of my hostlers. I have often overheard him praying and I know he can pray ; besides, I have watched his life and his temper, and I never saw anything in him inconsistent with Christian character ; call him in, I should be glad to hear him pray.

Tom comes slowly and modestly in, drops his hat at the door, looks on his sick and dying master. Tom, said the dying sceptic, do you ever pray ? do you know how to pray ? can you pray for your dying master and forgive him ? O yes, massa, with all my heart ; and drops on his knees and pours out a prayer for his soul.

Now the moral of this story is obvious. Place the sceptic on his dying bed, let that solemn hour arrive, and the inner convictions of his heart be revealed, and he knows of at least one man who is a Christian. He knows one man whose prayers he values more than all the friendship of all his former associates. He knows now that there is such a thing as Christianity ; and yet you cannot suppose that he has this moment learned a lesson he never knew before. No, he knew just as much before ; an honest hour has brought the inner convictions of his soul to light. Infidels generally know more than they have honesty enough to admit.

7. The great error of those who profess religion, but are not born of God, is this : they are trying to be Christians without being born of God. They need to have that done to them which is said of Adam—" God breathed into him the breath of life, and he became a living soul." Their religion has in it none of the breath of God : it is a cold, lifeless theory ; there is none of the living vitality of God in it. It is perhaps a heartless orthodoxy, and they may take a flattering

unction to their hearts that their creed is sound ; but do they *love* that truth which they profess to believe? They think, it may be, that they have zeal, and that their zeal is right and their heart right ; but is their soul on fire for God and His cause? Where are they, and what are they doing? Are they spinning out some fond theory, or defending it at the point of the sword? Ah, do they care for souls? Does their heart tremble for the interests of Zion? Do their very nerves quiver under the mighty power of God's truth? Does their love for God and for souls set their orthodoxy and their creeds *on fire* so that every truth burns in their souls and glows forth from their very faces? If so, then you will not see them absent from the prayer-meetings ; but you will see that divine things take hold of their soul with overwhelming interest and power. You will see them living Christians, burning and shining lights in the world. Brethren, it cannot be too strongly impressed on every mind that the decisive characteristic of true religion is energy, not apathy : that its vital essence is *life*, not *death*.

2

DEATH TO SIN

"Likewise reckon ye also yourselves to be dead indeed unto sin, but alive unto God through Jesus Christ our Lord." —Romans 6:11.

THE connection of this passage will help us to understand its meaning. Near the close of the previous chapter Paul had said—"The law entered that the offence might abound; but where sin abounded, grace did much more abound, that as sin hath reigned unto death, even so might grace reign through righteousness, unto eternal life, by Jesus Christ our Lord." He speaks here of sin as being a reigning principle or monarch, and of grace also as reigning. Then, in chapter vi., he proceeds—"What shall we say then? Shall we continue in sin that grace may abound? Likewise reckon ye also yourselves to be dead indeed unto sin, but alive unto God through Jesus Christ our Lord."

You observe here that Paul speaks of the man, the old sinner, as being *crucified with Christ*—so destroyed by the moral power of the Cross that he who was once a sinner shall no longer serve sin. When he speaks of our being planted or buried with Christ, we must of course understand him as employing figures of speech to teach the great truth that the *Gospel redeems the soul from sin*. *As* Christ died for sin, so by a general analogy we die to sin; while, on the other hand, as He rose to a new and infinitely glorious life, so the convert rises to a new and blessed life of purity and holiness.

But recurring particularly to our text, let me say—The language used in our translation would seem to denote that our death to sin is precisely analogous to Christ's death for sin; but this is not the case. We are dead to sin in the sense that it is no longer to be our master, implying that it *has* been in power over us. But sin never was in power over Jesus Christ—never was His master. Christ died to abolish its power over us—not to abolish any power of sin over Himself, for it had none. The analogy between Christ's death in relation to sin and our dying to sin, goes to this extent and no farther: He died for the sake of making an atonement for sin and of creating a moral power that should be effective to kill the love of sin in all hearts; but the Christian dies *unto* sin in the sense of being divorced from all sympathy with sin and emancipated from its control.

But I must proceed to remark upon the text itself, and shall inquire,—

I. *What it is to be dead unto sin* in the sense of the text.

II. *What it is to be alive unto God.*

III. *What it is to reckon ourselves to be dead unto sin, but alive unto God through Jesus Christ our Lord.*

IV. *What it is to be alive unto God through Jesus Christ.*

V. *What is implied in the exhortation of our text.*

I. Being dead *to* sin must obviously be the opposite of being dead *in* sin. The latter must undeniably be a state of entire sinfulness—a state in which the soul is dead to all good through the power of sin over it. But right over against this, to be *dead to sin,* must be to be indifferent to its attractions—beyond the reach of its influence—as fully removed from its influences as the dead are from the objects of sense in this world. As he who is dead in the natural sense has nothing more to do with earthly things, so he who is dead to sin has nothing to do any more with sin's attractions or with sinning itself.

II. *What is it to be alive unto God?* To be full of life for

Him—to be altogether active and on the alert to do His will; to make our whole lives a perpetual offering to Him, constantly delivering up ourselves to Him and His service that we may glorify His name and subserve His interests.

III. What is it to reckon ourselves dead indeed unto Him?

The word rendered *reckon* is sometimes rendered *account*. Abraham's faith was *accounted* unto him for righteousness. So, in this passage, reckon must mean—*believe, esteem* yourselves dead indeed unto sin. Account this to be the case. Regard this as truly your relation to sin; you are entirely dead to it; it shall have no more dominion over you.

A careful examination of the passages where this original word is used will show that this is its usual and natural sense. And this gives us the true idea of Gospel faith—embracing personally the salvation which is by faith in Jesus Christ. But more of this hereafter.

IV. What is meant by reckoning yourselves alive indeed unto God through Jesus Christ? Plainly this: that you are to expect to be saved by Jesus Christ and to calculate on this salvation as your own. You are to esteem yourself as wholly dead to sin and as consequently brought into life and peace in Christ Jesus.

V. *What is implied in the exhortation of our text?*

That there is an adequate provision for this expectation, and for realizing these blessings in fact. For if there were no ground for realization this, the injunction would be most absurd. A precept requiring us to account ourselves dead indeed unto sin and alive unto God, would be utterly untenable if there were no probability of the thing—if no provision were made for our coming into such relations to sin on the one hand and to God through Christ on the other. For if these blessings could not be reasonably expected, there could be no rational ground for the expectation. If it were not reasonable to expect it, then to enjoin us to expect it would be palpably unreasonable. Who does not see that the very injunction implies that there is a foundation laid and adequate provision made for the state required ?

What is implied in complying with this injunction ?

1. Believing such a thing to be possible. Believing it possible that through Christ we may live in the required manner, that we may avoid sin—desist from sinning—give it up and abandon it altogether, and put it forever away. There can be no such thing as an intelligent compliance with this precept, except as there shall underlie it this belief in its practicability. A state actually made practicable by adequate grace, adapted to the laws of mind and to the actual moral condition of lost men.

2. That we cease from all expectation of attaining this state of ourselves, and by our own independent, unaided efforts. There is no beginning to receive by grace till we renounce all expectation of attaining by natural works. It is only when empty of self that we begin to be filled of Christ.

3. A present willingness to be saved from sin. We must actually renounce all sin *as such*—that is, renounce sin because it is sin, and for what it is. This position the mind must take : I can have nothing more to do with sinning—for God hates sin, and I am to live henceforth and for ever to please and glorify Him. My soul is committed with its utmost strength of purpose to this pleasing of God and doing His will.

4. It implies also an entire committal of your whole case to Jesus Christ, not only for present, but for all future salvation from sin. This is absolutely essential. It must always be the vital step—the cardinal act in this great work of salvation from sin.

5. It implies also the foreclosing of the mind against temptation, in such a sense that the mind truly expects to live a life purely devoted to God. This is the same sort of foreclosing of the mind as takes place under a faithful marriage

contract. The Bible everywhere keeps this figure prominent. Christians are represented as the *bride* of Christ. They stand in a relation to Him which is closely analogous to that of a bride to her husband. Hence when they commit their whole hearts to Him, reposing their affections in Him, and trusting Him for all good, their hearts are strongly foreclosed against temptation. The principle here involved, we see illustrated in the merely human relation. When parties are solemnly betrothed in mutual honest fidelity, there is no longer any thought of letting the eye rove or the heart go abroad for a fresh object of interest and love. The heart is fixed— willingly and by plighted faith *fixed*, and this fact shuts out the power of temptation almost entirely. It renders it comparatively an easy matter to keep the heart safely above the influence of temptation to apostasy. Before the sacred vows are taken, individuals may be excused for looking round and making any observations or inquiries : but never *after* the solemn vow is made. After the parties have become *one* by vow of marriage, never to be broken, there is to be no more question as to a better choice—no further thought about changing the relation or withdrawing the heart's affections. No wavering is admissible now ; the pledge is made for *everlasting* faithfulness, settled once and forever ! This is God's own illustration, and surely none need be more apt or more forcible. It shows how the Christian should look upon sin and upon all temptation to sin. He must say, *Away from my heart for ever !* I am married to Jesus Christ ; how then can I look after other lovers ? My mind is forever settled. It rests in the deep repose of one whose affections are plighted and fixed—to rove no more ! Sin ? I can think of yielding to its seductions no longer. I cannot entertain the question for a moment. I can have nothing to do with sinning. My mind is settled—the question forever foreclosed, and I can no more admit the temptation to small sins than to great sins—no more consent to give my heart to worldly idols than to commit murder! I did not enter upon religion as upon an experiment, to see how I might like it— no more than a wife or husband take on themselves the marriage vow as an experiment. No; my whole soul has committed itself to Jesus Christ with as much expectation of being faithful forever as the most faithful husband and wife have of fulfilling their vows in all fidelity till death shall part them.

Christians in this state of mind no more expect to commit small sins than great sins. Hating all sin for its own sake and for its hatefulness to Christ, any sin, however small, is to them as murder. Hence if the heart is ever afterwards seduced and overcome by temptation, it is altogether contrary to their expectation and purpose; it was not embraced in their plan by any means, but was distinctly excluded; it was not deliberately indulged aforetime, but broke on them unexpectedly through the vantage ground of old habits or associations.

Again, the state of mind in question implies that the Christian knows where his great strength lies. He knows it does not lie in works of fasting, giving alms, making prayers, doing public duties or private duties—nothing of this sort; not even in resolutions or any self-originated efforts, but only in Christ received by faith. He no more expects spiritual life of himself apart from Christ, than a man in his senses would expect to fly by swinging his arms in the air. Deep in his soul lies the conviction that his whole strength lies in Christ alone.

When men are so enlightened as truly to apprehend this subject, then to expect less than this from Jesus Christ as the result of committing the whole soul to Him for full salvation, is virtually to reject Him as a revealed Saviour. It does not honour Him for what He is; it does not honour the revelations He has made of Himself in His word by accepting Him as there presented. For consider, what is the first element of this salvation? Not being saved from hell, but being saved from *sin*. Salvation from punishment is quite a secondary thing, in every sense. It is only a *result* of being saved from sin, and not the prime element in the Gospel salvation. Why was the infant Messiah to be called Jesus? Because He should *save His people from their sins*. And does the Bible anywhere teach any other or different view from this?

CONCLUSION

1. This text alone—" Reckon yourselves to be dead indeed unto sin, but alive unto God through Jesus Christ "—most entirely justifies the expectation of living without sin through all-abounding grace. If there were no other passage bearing on this point, this alone is adequate, and for a Christian to offer this only as a reason for such a hope in Him is to offer as good a reason as need be given. There are indeed many others that fully justify this expectation.

2. To teach that such an expectation is a dangerous error is to teach unbelief. What if the apostle had added to this injunction which requires us to account ourselves dead indeed unto sin, but alive unto God, this singular averment : " Yet let me warn you, nobody can rationally hope to be free from sin in this world. You must remember that to entertain such an expectation as God enjoins in this language is a dangerous error." What should be thought of this if it were attached to Rom. vi. 11 ?

No man can deny that the passage treats of sanctification. The whole question is, Shall Christians " *continue in sin* " after having been forgiven and accepted in their Redeemer ? Paul labours to show that they *should*, and of course that they *may* die to sin—even as Christ died for sin ; and may also live a new, a spiritual life (through faith in His grace), even as Christ does a higher and more glorious life.

Let me refer here to another passage, in which it is said— " Be not unequally yoked with unbelievers—what agreement hath the temple of God with idols? For ye are the temple of the living God. Wherefore come out from among them and be ye separate, saith the Lord, and touch not the unclean thing, and I will receive you, and will be a Father unto you, and ye shall be my sons and daughters, saith the Lord Almighty." "Having, therefore, these promises, dearly beloved, let us cleanse ourselves from all filthiness of the flesh and of the spirit, perfecting holiness in the fear of God."—2 Cor. vi. 11—18, and vii. 1. This is a very remarkable passage. Note how precept and promise are intermingled, and how, finally, upon the basis of a most glorious promise, is founded the precept enjoining us to *perfect holiness.* Now what should we think of Paul and of the Divine Spirit who spake through Paul, if He had immediately subjoined—"Take care lest any of you should be led by these remarks to indulge the very dangerous and erroneous expectation that you can "perfect holiness," or "cleanse yourselves from any sin, either of flesh or spirit, in this world?" Would not this have been trifling with the intelligence and Christian sensibility of every reader of his words throughout all time? Should we not account it as substantially blasphemous?

It so happens that the Bible never gainsays its own teachings; but I ask—What if it had? What if the Bible had solemnly asserted—"No mere man, either of himself or by any grace received in this life, has ever kept or shall ever keep the commandments of God wholly, but doth daily break them in thought, word, and deed?"

To teach that such an expectation is dangerous is a great deal worse than no teaching at all. Far better to leave men to their own unaided reading of God's word, for this could scarcely in any case so sadly mislead them, however inclined they might be to the misapprehension. Dangerous to expect salvation from sin? Dangerous? What does this mean? What! Dangerous to expect victory over any sin? If so, what is the Gospel worth? What Gospel have we that can be deemed *good news* at all?

Many indulge the very opposite expectation. Far from expecting any such thing as the apostle authorizes them to expect, they know they have no such expectation.

Of some yet more than this is true—they expect to count themselves always in sin. They depend on reckoning themselves, not dead indeed unto sin, but somewhat alive to it through all their mortal life, and in part alive to God through Jesus Christ. It follows as quite a thing of course that expecting no such thing as complete victory over sin they will use no appropriate means, since *faith* stands foremost among those means, and faith must include at least a confidence that the thing sought is possible to be attained.

In this and the following chapters we have the essence of the good news of the Gospel. Any one who has been wounded and made sore by sin—its bitter shafts sinking deep into his moral being—one who has known its bitterness and felt the poison thereof drink up his spirit—such an one will see that there is glory in the idea of being delivered from sin. He will surely see that this deliverance is by far the greatest want of his soul, and that nothing can be compared with escaping from this body of sin and death. Look at Rom. vii. There you will have the state of a man who is more than convinced, who is really *convicted*. It is one thing to be convinced, and a yet further stage of progress in the right direction to be convicted. This term implies the agency of another party. The criminal at the bar may be quite convinced of his guilt by the view he was compelled to take of his own case; but his being *convicted* is a still further step; the testimony and the jury *convict* him.

Some of you know what it is to see yourself a sinner, and yet the sight of the fact brings with it no smart—no sting; it does not cut deep into your very soul. On the other hand, some of you may know what it is to see your sins all armed like an armed man to pierce you through and through with daggers. Then you cry out as here—O wretched man that I am! Who shall deliver me from the body of this death? You feel a piercing sting as if your soul were filled with poison—with dark rankling venom, diffusing through the depths of your soul the very agonies of hell! This is what I mean by being convicted, as a state of mind beyond being merely convinced. The shafts and the smiting of sin seem really like the piercings of an arrow, as if arrows from the Almighty did really drink up your spirit. When you experience this, then you can understand what the good news of the Gospel is. A remedy for such pangs must be good news beyond all contradiction. Then to know that the blood of Christ can save, is indeed a cordial of life to the fainting soul.

Place a man in this state of cutting, piercing conviction, and then let him feel that there is actually no remedy, and he sinks under the iron shafts of despair. See his agony! Tell him there can never be any remedy for his guilty soul! You must lie there in you wailing and despair forever! Can any state of mind be more awful?

I remember a case that occurred in Reading, Pa., many years ago. There was a man of hard heart and iron frame— a strong, burly man, who had stood up against the revival as if he could shake off all the arrows of the Almighty, even as the Mastodon of which the tradition of the red man says, He shook off all the arrows of the warriors from his brow and felt no harm. So he stood. But he had a praying wife and a praying sister, and they gathered their souls in the might of prayer close about him as a party of men would hem in a wild bull in a net. Soon it was apparent that an arrow from the quiver of the Almighty had pierced between the joints of his harness and had taken hold of his innermost heart. O, was not he in agony then! It was night—dark and intensely cold. It seemed that absolutely he could not live. They sent for me to come and see him. I went. While yet sixty rods from his house I heard his screams and wailings of woe. It made me feel awfully solemn—so like the echoes of the pit of hell ! I reached the house : there he lay on the floor rolling in his agony and wailing, such as is rarely heard this side the pit of despair. Cold as the weather was, he sweat like rain, every part of his frame being in a most intense perspiration. Oh, his groans ! and to see him gnaw his very tongue for pain —this could not but give one some idea of the doom of the damned. O, said I, if this be only conviction, *what is hell?* But he could not bear to hear anything about sin ; his conscience was already full of it, and had brought out the awful things of God's law so as to leave nothing more to be done in that direction. I could only put Christ before him, and just hold his mind to the view of Christ alone. This soon brought relief. But suppose I had nothing else to say but this—" Mr. B., there is no help possible for your case ! You can wail on and wail on : no being in the universe can help you ?" Need you say to him hell has no fire ? Oh, he has fire enough in his burning soul already. It seems to him that no hell of fire can possibly be worse than this.

How perfectly chilling and horrible for persons to oppose the idea of expecting deliverance from sin and yet talk calmly of going on in sin all the rest of their earthly days ! As an elder whom I knew rose in meeting and told the Lord he had been living in sin thus far, and expected to go on in sin as long as he lived ; he had sinned to-day and should doubtless sin to-morrow and so on—and yet he talked as calmly about it all as if it were foolish to make any ado, as well as impossible to attempt any change for the better. Talk of all this calmly—think of that ! Quite calmly of living alone in sin all the rest of his days ! How horrible ! Suppose a wife should say to her husband, " I love you some, but you know I love many other men too, and that I find it pleasant to

indulge myself with them.   You certainly must be aware that
all women are frail creatures, and liable to fall continually,
and indeed you know that I expect to fall more or less, as it
may happen, every day I live, so that you certainly will not
expect from me anything so impracticable and fanatical as
unblemished virtue !   You know we have none of us any idea
of being perfect in the present life—we don't believe in any
such thing ! "

Now let me ask you to look at this woman and hear what
she has to say.   Can you hear her talk so, without having
your soul filled with horror ?   What ! is this woman a *wife*,
and does she think and talk in this way about conjugal
fidelity ?

And yet this is not to be compared in shocking guilt and
treason with the case of the Christian who says, "I expect
to sin every day I live," and who says this with unmoved
carelessness.   You expect to be a traitor to Jesus each day
of your life ; to crucify Him afresh each day ; to put Him
each day to an open shame ; each day to dishonour His name,
and grieve His heart, and to bring sorrow and shame upon
all who love Christ's cause ; and yet you talk about having a
good hope through grace !   But tell me, does not every true
Christian say, "Do not let me live at all if I cannot live
without sin ; for how can I bear to go on day by day sinning
against Him whom I so much love !"

Those who are really opposed to this idea, are either very
ignorant of what the Gospel is, or they are impenitent and
of course do not care to be delivered from their sins ; or at
best they are guilty of great unbelief.   Into which of these
classes the opposers of the doctrine may fall, is a question
for themselves to settle, as between their own consciences and
their God.

There are two distinct views of salvation entertained
among professed Christians, and correspondingly two distinct classes of professors—often embraced within the same

church. The one class regard the Gospel as a salvation from sin. They think more of this and value it more than the hope of heaven, or of earth either. The great thing with them is to realize the idea of deliverance from sin. This constitutes the charm and glory of the Gospel. They seek this more than to be saved from hell. They care more by far to be saved from sin itself than from its penal consequences. Of the latter they think and pray but little. It is their glory and their joy that Christ is sent to deliver them from their bondage in iniquity—to lift them up from their wretched state and give them the liberty of love. This they labour to realize; this is to them the good news of Gospel salvation.

The other class are mostly anxious to be saved from hell. The punishment due for sin is the thing they chiefly fear. In fact, fear has been mainly the spring of their religious efforts. The Gospel is not thought of as a means of deliverance from sin, but as a great system of *indulgences*—a vast accommodation to take off the fear and danger of damnation, while yet it leaves them in their sin. Now, here I do not by any means imply that they will call their system of Gospel faith a scheme of indulgences: the name doubtless will be an offence to them. They may not have distinctly considered this point, and may have failed to notice that in fact it is such and nothing better.

They seem not to notice that a scheme of salvation that removes the fear of damnation for sin, and which yet leaves them in their sins to live for themselves, to please themselves, and which holds that Christ will at last bring them to heaven notwithstanding their having lived in sin all their days, must be a *vast scheme of indulgences*. Indeed, it is a *compromise* on a most magnificent scale. By virtue of it, the whole Church is expected to wallow on in sin through life, and be none the less sure of heaven at last.

These opposite views are so prevalent and so palpable you

will see them everywhere as you go round among the
churches. You will find many in the Church who are
altogether worldly and selfish; who live conformed to the
world in various neglects of duty, and who expect to indulge
themselves in sin more or less all the way through life. You
may ask them—Do you think that is right? They answer—
No. Why, then, do you do it? Oh, we are all imperfect, and
we can't expect to be any better than imperfect, while here in
the flesh. Yet they expect to be saved at last from hell, and
to have all their sins forgiven; but how? Not on condition
of sincerely turning away from all their sins, but on the
assumption that the Gospel is a vast system of indulgences—
more vast by far than Pope Leo X. ever wielded and worked
to comfort sinning professors in his day. For here are not
merely those that sin *occasionally* as *there*, but those who
live in sin and know they do, and expect they shall as long
as they live, yet expect to be saved without fail at last.

The other class of professed Christians have no expectation
of being saved only as they have a pure heart and live above
the world. Talk to them about living in sin, they hate
and dread the very thought. To them the poison of asps
is in it. Sin is bitter to their souls. They dread it as they
dread death itself.

No one can go round within this church or any other
without finding these two classes as distinct in their appre-
hension of the Gospel as I have described them to be. The
one class are in agony if they find themselves even slipping,
and they are specially cautious against exposing themselves
to temptation.

Not so with the other class. Two ministers of the Gospel being together, one urged the other strongly to engage in
a certain service. The other declined. "Why not go?"
said the first. "Because I do not think myself justified in
exposing myself to such and so much temptation."

"But why stop for that? We expect to sin more or less

always; and all we have to do is to repent of it after-wards."

Horror-smitten, the other could only say, "I hold to a different Gospel from that altogether."

Suppose a wife should say to her husband, "I am deter-mined I will go to the theatre." "But, my dear," says he, "you know bad people congregate there, and you may be tempted." But she replies, "Never mind; if I sin I will repent of it afterwards."

The real Christian may be known by this, that the very thought of being drawn into sin drives him to agony. He cannot bear the idea of living in sin; no, not for one moment.

The young people here who are truly Christians, are care-ful about this ensuing vacation. You will be on your guard, for you are afraid you may be ensnared into sin. I do not mean that you need fear to go where God calls you, but it is a terrible thing to be ensnared into sin, and you cannot but feel it to be so. If you know what it is to be wounded by the arrows of sin in your soul, you will go abroad into apparent danger, walking softly and with caution, and much prayer. You will surely be much on your guard. But if you say, "Oh, if I sin I will repent," what shall I say of you? You will repent will you? And this will make all right again so easily? Suppose you foresaw that in going abroad for vacation you would get drunk a few times, and would commit one or two murders, would you say, "Oh, I may be a good Christian notwithstanding. I will be careful to repent of it after it is all over." *Horrible!* And yet you can think yourself a good Christian! Let me tell you, a Christian man who repents of sin, repents of it *as* sin. He makes no such discriminations as between a little secret sin and a great sin—for example, a murder. He knows no such distinction between sins as will leave him to commit the one class without scruple and to shrink from the other. With him anything that grieves God is a horrible thing. Anything that displeases God—" Ah," he cries out, " God will see it ; it will grieve His heart !" How it will affect God—this is all in all with him. One who knows what it is to appear guilty of sin before God, and then who knows also what it is to be delivered from this condition, will understand how the Christian ought to feel in circumstances of temptation, where he feels himself in danger of sinning. His hair all stands on end ! How awful to sin against God ! Hence, anything that seems likely to bring him into danger will rouse up all his soul within him, and put him on his guard.

The unbelief of the Church as to what they may receive from Christ is the great stumbling-block, hindering themselves and others from experiencing deliverance. Not only is this a great curse to professed Christians, but it is also a great grief to Jesus Christ and a sore trial.

Many seem to have hardened their hearts against all expectation of this deliverance from sin. They have heard the doctrine preached. They have seen some profess to be in this state of salvation from sin, but they have also seen some of this class fall again, and now they deliberately reject the whole doctrine. But is this consistent with really embracing the Gospel ? What is Christ to the believer ? What was His errand into the world ? What is He doing, and what is He trying to do ?

He has come to break the power of sin in the heart, and to be the life of the believer, working in him a perpetual salvation from sin, aiming to bring him thus, and only thus, to heaven at last. What is faith ? what but the actual giving of yourself up to Christ that He may do this work for you and in you ? What are you to believe of Christ if not this, that He is to save His people from their sins ? Can you tell of anything else ? Does the Bible tell you to expect something different and less than this ? The fact is, that it has been the great stumbling-block to the Church that this thing has not been well understood. The common experience of nominal Christians has misrepresented and belied the truth. The masses forming their views much more from this experience than from the Bible, or at best applying this experience to interpret the Bible, have adopted exceedingly defective, not to say false, opinions as to the nature and design of the Gospel. They seem to forget altogether that Paul, writing to Christians at Rome, assures them that if they are under grace, sin shall not have dominion over them.

When Christians do not expect this blessing from Christ, they will not get it. While they expect so little as they usually do, no wonder they get so little. According to their faith, and not ever very much beyond it, need they expect to receive.

It is often the case that sanctification is held as a theory, while the mind does not yet by any means embrace the truth in love. The case is analogous to that of impenitent sinners who hold in theory that they must have a new heart. They profess to believe thus, but do they really understand it?' No. Suppose it were revealed to their minds so that they should really see it as it is, would they not see a new thing? Would they not be startled to see how utterly far they are, while impenitent, from being acceptable to God, and how great the change they must experience before they can enter the kingdom? So of sanctification. Although this class of persons profess to hold it in theory, yet the passages of Scripture which describe it do not enter into their experience. They do not see the whole truth. If they were to see the whole truth, and should then reject it, I believe it would be in them the unpardonable sin. When the Spirit of God discloses to them the real meaning of the Gospel, then if they deliberately reject it, how can the sin be less than what the Scriptures represent as the unpardonable sin? Having once been enlightened, and having received the knowledge of the truth that they might be saved, then turning back, is it not thenceforth impossible that they should be renewed again to repentance ?   One thing, at least, must be said, there is a peril which many of the professed Christians of our day seem not to realize, in having so much light before the mind as they actually have in regard to the provisions made in the Gospel for present sanctification, and then in rejecting this light practically and living still in sin as if the Gospel made no provision to save the Christian from his sins. Into this awful peril how many rush blindly and to their own destruction !

3

DISHONESTY IN SMALL MATTERS

"He that is unjust in the least is unjust also in much." —Luke 16:10b.

THESE words are a part of the parable of the unjust steward, or rather, a principle which our Lord lays down in connection with the parable. The words do not require that I should go into an explanation of the parable itself, as they make no part of the story which the Lord Jesus was relating. The PRINCIPLE involved or laid down is what I have to do with to-night. In preaching from these words I design to illustrate the principle laid down, which is this:

One who is dishonest in small matters, is not really honest in anything.

The order which I shall pursue is the following:

I. I shall show what I do not mean by this principle.

II. Show what I do mean by it.

III. Prove the principle, that one who is dishonest in small matters is not really honest at all.

IV. Show by what principle those individuals are governed who, while they are dishonest in small things, appear to be honest, and even religious, in larger affairs.

V. Mention several instances where persons often manifest a want of principle in small matters.

I. I am to show what I do not mean by the principle, that one who is dishonest in small matters is not really honest in anything.

Answer. I do not mean that if a person is dishonest in small matters, and will take little advantages in dealing,

46

it is therefore certain that in greater matters he will not deal openly and honorably according to the rules of business.

Or that it is certain, if a man will commit petty thefts and depredations, that he will commit highway robbery. There may be various reasons why a man who will commit such depredations will not go into more daring and outrageous crimes.

Or that if a man indulges unclean thoughts, it is certain he will commit adultery.

Or that if he indulges covetous desires, it is certain he will steal.

Or that if he indulges in ill-will towards any one, he will commit murder.

Or that if he would enslave a fellow man, and deprive him of instruction and of all the rights of man, he will certainly commit other crimes of equal enormity.

Or that if he will defraud the government in little things, such as postage, or duties on little articles, he will rob the treasury.

II. I am to explain what I do mean by the principle laid down, that if a man is dishonest in little things, he is not really honest in anything.

What I mean is, that if a man is dishonest in small matters, it shows that he is not governed by principle in anything. It is therefore certain that it is not real honesty of heart which leads him to act right in greater matters. He must have other motives than honesty of heart, if he appears to act honestly in larger things, while he acts dishonestly in small matters.

III. I am to prove the principle.

I am not going to take it for granted, although the Lord Jesus Christ expressly declares it. I design to mention several considerations in addition to the force of the text. I believe it is a general impression that a person may be honest in greater matters, and deserve the character of honesty, notwithstanding he is guilty of dishonesty in small matters.

1. If he was actuated by a supreme regard to the authority of God and if this was the habitual state of his mind, such a state of mind would be quite as apt to manifest itself in smaller matters as in large. Nay, where the temptation is small, he would be more certain to act conscientiously than in greater matters, because there is less to induce him to act otherwise. What is honesty? If a man has no other motives for acting honestly than mere selfishness, the devil is as honest as he is; for I dare say he is honest with his fellow devils, as far as it is for his interest or policy to be so. Is that honesty? Certainly not. And, therefore, if a man does not act honestly from higher motives than this, he is not honest at all, and if he appears to be honest in certain important matters, he has other motives than a regard to the honor of God.

2. It is certain that, if an individual is dishonest in small matters, he is not actuated by love to God. If he was actuated by love to God, he would feel that dishonesty in small matters is just as inconsistent as in great. It is as real a violation of the law of God, and one who truly loves God would no more act dishonestly in one than in the other.

3. It is certain that he is not actuated by real love to his neighbour, such as the law of God requires. If he loved his neighbor as himself, he would not defraud him in small things any more than in great. Nay, he might do it in great things, where the temptation to swerve from his integrity was powerful. But where the temptation is small, it cannot be that one who truly loves his neighbor would act dishonestly. See the case of Job. Job truly loved God, and you see how far he went, and what distress he endured, before he would say a word that even seemed disparaging

or complaining of God. And when the temptation was overwhelming, and he could see no reason why he should be so afflicted, and his distress became intolerable, and his soul was all in darkness, and his wife set in and told him to curse God and die, he would not do it then, but said, "Thou speakest as one of the foolish women speaketh. What! shall we receive good at the hand of God, and shall we not receive evil?" Do you suppose Job would have swerved from his integrity in little things, or for small temptations? Never. He loved God. And if you find a man who truly loves his neighbor, you will not see him deceiving or defrauding his neighbor for trifling temptations.

IV. I am to examine some of the motives by which a person may be actuated, who is dishonest in little things, while he may appear to be honest in greater matters.

Our own business here is to ascertain how this apparent discrepancy can consist with the declaration in the text. The Lord Jesus Christ has laid down the principle, that if a man is dishonest in small matters, he is not strictly honest at all. Now, here are facts, which to many appear to contradict this. We see many men that in small matters exhibit a great want of principle, and appear to be quite void of principle, while in larger things they appear to be honorable and even pious. This must be consistent, or else Jesus Christ has affirmed a falsehood. That it is consistent with truth will be admitted, if we can show that their conduct in regard to larger matters can be accounted for on other principles than honesty of heart. If we can account for it on principles of mere selfishness, it will be admitted, that where a man is dishonest in small things, he is not really honest at all, however honestly he may act in regard to larger matters.

1. They may act honestly in larger matters for fear of disgrace.

They may know that certain small things are not likely to be mentioned in public, or to have a noise made about them, and so they may do such things, while the fear of disgrace deters them from doing the same things in regard to larger matters, because it will make a noise. What is this but one form of selfishness overbalancing another form? It is selfishness still, not honesty.

2. He may suppose it will injure his business, if he is guilty of dishonesty with men of business, and so he deals honestly in important matters, while in little things he is ready to take any advantage he can, that will not injure his business. Thus a man will take advantage of a seamstress, and pay her a little less than he knows it is really worth for making a garment, while the same individual, in buying a bale of goods, would not think of showing a disposition to cheat, because it would injure his business. In dealing with an abused and humble individual, he can gripe and screw out a few cents without fear of public disgrace, while he would not for any consideration do an act which would be publicly spoken of as disreputable and base.

3. Fear of human law may influence a man to act honestly in such things as are likely to be taken up, while in such small matters as the law is not likely to notice, he will defraud or take advantage.

4. The love of praise influences many to act honestly and honorably, and even piously, in matters that are likely to be noticed. Many a man will defraud a poor person out of a few cents in the price of labor, and then, in some great matter on a public occasion, appear to act with great liberality. What is the reason, that individuals who habitually screw down their servants, and seamstresses, and other poor people that they employ, to the lowest penny, and take all the advantage they can of such people, will then, if a severe winter comes, send out cart loads of fuel

to the poor, or give large sums of money to the commit-
tees? You see that it is for the love of praise, and not for
the love of God nor the love of man.

5. The fear of God. He may be afraid of the divine
wrath, if he commits dishonest acts of importance, while
he supposes God will overlook little things, and not notice
it if he is dishonest in such small matters.

6. He may restrain his dishonest propensities from
mere self-righteousness, and act honestly in great things,
for the sake of bolstering up his own good opinion of
himself, while in little things he will cheat and play the
knave.

I said in the beginning, that I did not mean, that if a
man would take small advantages, he would certainly never
act with apparent uprightness. It often comes to pass,
that individuals who act with great meanness and dishonesty in small affairs, will act uprightly and honorably, on
the ground that their character and interest are at stake.
Many a man, who among merchants is looked upon as an
honorable dealer, is well known, by those who are more in-
timately acquainted with him, to be mean and knavish and
overreaching in smaller matters, or in his dealings with
more humble and more dependent individuals. It is plain
that it is not real honesty of heart which makes him act
with apparent honesty in his more public transactions.

So I said, that if an individual will commit petty thefts,
it is not certain he would commit highway robbery. He
might have various reasons for abstaining, without having
a particle too much honesty to rob on the highway, or to
cut a purse out of your pocket in a crowd. The individual may not have courage enough to break out in highway
robbery, or not skill enough, or nerve enough, or he may
be afraid of the law, or afraid of disgrace, or other reasons.

An individual may indulge unclean thoughts, habitually, and yet never actually commit adultery. He may be

restrained by fear, or want of opportunity, and not by principle. If he *indulges* unclean thoughts, he would certainly act uncleanly, if it were not for other reasons than purity of principle.

An individual may manifest a covetous spirit, and yet not steal. But he has the spirit that would lead him to steal, if not restrained by other reasons than honesty or principle.

A man may be angry, and yet his anger never break out in murder. But his hatred would lead him to do it, so far as principle is concerned. And if it is not done, it is for other reasons than true principle.

An individual may oppress his fellow man, enslave him, deprive him of instruction, and compel him to labor without compensation, for his own benefit, and yet not commit murder, or go to Africa to engage in the slave trade, because it would endanger his reputation or his life. But if he will do that which divests life of all that is desirable to gratify his own pride or promote his own interest, it cannot be principle, either of love to God or love to man, that keeps him from going any length, if his interest requires it. If a man, from regard to his own selfish interest, will take a course towards any human being which will deprive him of all that renders life desirable, it is easy to see that, so far as principle is concerned, there is nothing in the way of his doing it by violence on the coast of Africa or taking life itself when his interest requires it.

So an individual who will defraud the United States treasury of eighteen cents in postage has none too much principle to rob the treasury if he had the same prospect of impunity. The same principle that allowed him to do the one would allow him to do the other. And the same motive that led him to do the one, would lead him to do the other if he had an opportunity, and if it were not counteracted by some other motive equally selfish.

A man may, in like manner, be guilty of little misrepresentations, who would not dare to tell a downright *lie*. Yet if he is guilty of coloring the truth, and misrepresenting facts, with a design to deceive, or to make facts appear otherwise than they really are, he is really lying, and the individual who will do this would manufacture ever so many lies, if it was for his interest, or were he not restrained by other reasons than a sacred regard to truth.

V. I will mention some instances, where persons are dishonest in small matters, while they appear to act honestly and even piously in regard to matters of greater importance.

1. We often find individuals manifesting a great want of principle in regard to the payment of small debts, while they are extremely careful and punctual in the payment of notes in the bank, and in all their commercial transactions.

For instance, there is a man takes a newspaper, the price is only a small sum, and the publisher cannot send a collector to every individual, so this man lets his subscription lie along perhaps for years, and perhaps never pays it. The same individual, if it had been a note at the bank, would have been punctual enough; and no pains would have been spared, rather than let the note run beyond the day. Why? Because, if he does not pay his note in the bank, it will be protested, and his credit will be injured, but the little debt of twenty shillings or five dollars will not be protested, and he knows it, and so he lets it go by, and the publisher has to be at the trouble and expense of sending for it, or go without his money. How manifest it is that this man does not pay his notes at the bank from honesty of principle, but purely from a regard to his own credit and interest.

2. I have before referred to the case of seamstresses. Suppose an individual employs women to sew for him, and

for the sake of underselling others in the same trade, he beats down these women below the just price of such work. It is manifest that the individual is not honest in anything. If, for sake of making more profits, or of underselling, he will beat down these women—suppose he is honorable and prompt in his public transactions—no thanks to him, it is not because he is honest in his heart, but because it is his interest to seem so.

3. Some manifest this want of principle by committing little petty thefts. If they live at a boarding house, where there are boarders, they will commit little petty thefts—perhaps for fuel in the cellar. An individual will not be at the expense of getting a little charcoal for himself, to kindle his fire in the morning, but gets along by pilfering from the stores laid in by others, a handful at a time. Now the individual that will do that, shows himself to be radically rotten at heart.

A case came to my knowledge, of this kind. An individual was sitting in a room, where a gentleman had on the table for some purpose a tumbler of wine and a pitcher of water. The gentleman had occasion to go out of the room a moment, but accidentally left the door a-jar, and while he was out, looking back he saw this individual drink a part of the wine in the tumbler, and then, to conceal it, fill up the tumbler with water, and take his seat. Now the individual who did that showed that he loved wine, and that he was none too good to steal; he showed, that so far as principle was concerned, he would get drunk if he had the means, and steal if he had a chance; in fact, at heart, he was both a drunkard and a thief.

4. Individuals often manifest great dishonesty when they find articles that have been lost, especially articles of small value. One will find a penknife, perhaps, or a pencil case, and never make the least inquiry, even among those he has reason to believe were the losers. Now, the

man that would find a penknife, and keep it without making inquiry, where there was any prospect of finding the owner, so far as principle is concerned, would keep a pocket-book full of bank notes, if he should find it, and have an equal chance of concealment. And yet this same individual, if he should find a pocket-book with five thousand dollars in it, would advertise it in the newspapers, and make a great noise, and profess to be wonderfully honest. But what is his motive? He knows that the five thousand dollars will be inquired into, and if he is discovered to have concealed it, he shall be ruined. Fine honesty, this.

5. Many individuals conceal little mistakes that are made in their favor, in reckoning, or giving change. If an individual would keep still, say nothing, and let it pass, when such a mistake is made in his favor, it is manifest that nothing but a want of opportunity and impunity would prevent him from taking any advantage whatever, or overreaching to any extent.

6. Frauds on the post-office are of the same class.

Who does not know that there is a great deal of dishonesty practiced here? Some seem to think there is no dishonesty in cheating the government out of a little postage. Postmasters will frank letters they have no right to. Many will frank letters not only for their families but for their neighbors, all directly contrary to law, and a fraud upon the post-office. The man that will do that is not honest. What would not such a man do, if he had the same prospect of impunity in other frauds, that he has in this?

7. Smuggling is a common form of petty dishonesty. How many a man will contrive to smuggle little articles in his trunk, when he comes home from England, that he knows ought to pay duty to the custom-house, and he thinks but little of it, because the sum is so small; where-

as, the smaller the sum the more clearly is principle developed. *Because* the temptation is so small, it shows how weak is the man's principle of honesty, that can be overcome by such a trifle. The man that would do this, if he had the same opportunity, would smuggle a cargo. If, for so little, he would lose sight of his integrity, and do a dishonest act, he is not too good to rob the treasury.

CONCLUSION

1. The real state of a man's heart is often more manifested in smaller matters than in business of greater moment.

Men are often deceived here, and think their being honest in greater things will go to prove their honesty of heart, notwithstanding their knavishness in smaller things, and so they are sure to be on their guard in great things, while they are careless of little matters, and so act out their true character. They overlook the fact, that all their honesty in larger matters springs from a wrong principle, from a desire "to appear" honest, and not from a determination to be honest. They overlook their own petty frauds because they guard their more public manifestations of character, and then take it for granted that they are honest, while they are nothing but rottenness at heart. The man who will take advantage in little things, where he is not watched, is not actuated by principle. If you want to know your real character, watch your hearts, and see how your principles develop themselves in little things.

For instance, suppose you are an eye-servant. You are employed in the service of another, and you do not mind being idle at times for a short time, in the absence of your employer. Or you slight your work when not under the eye of your employer, as you would not if he was present. The man who will do this is totally dishonest, and not to be trusted in any thing, and very likely would take money from his employer's pocket-book, if it were not for the fear of detection or some other equally selfish motive. Such a person is not to be trusted at all, except in circumstances where it is his interest to be honest.

Mechanics that slight their work when it will not be seen or known by their employer, are rotten at heart, and not to be trusted at all, any farther than you can make it for their interest to be honest.

Persons who will knowingly misstate facts in conversation, would bear false witness in court under oath, if favored with opportunity and impunity. They never tell the truth at all because it is truth, or from the love of truth. Let no such men be trusted.

Those who are unchaste in conversation would be unchaste in conduct, if they had opportunity and impunity. Spurn the man or woman who will be impure in speech, even among their own sex, they have no principle at all, and are not to be trusted on the ground of their principles. If persons are chaste from principle, they will no more indulge in unclean conversation than unclean actions. They will abhor even the garment spotted with the flesh.

2. The individual who will indulge in any one sin, does not abstain from any sin because it is sin.

If he hated sin, and was opposed to sin because it is sin, he would no more indulge in one sin than another. If a person goes to pick and choose among sins, avoiding some, and practicing others, it is certain that it is not because he regards the authority of God, or hates sin, that he abstains from any sin whatever.

3. Those individuals who will not abandon all intoxicating drinks for the purpose of promoting temperance, never gave up ardent spirits for the sake of promoting temperance.

It is manifest that they gave up ardent spirits from

some other consideration than a regard to the temperance cause. If that had been their object, they would give up alcohol in all its forms, and when they find that there is alcohol in wine, and beer, and cider they would give them up of course. Why not?

4. The man who for the sake of gain, will sell rum, or intoxicating drinks, to his neighbor, and put a cup to his neighbor's mouth, and would thus consent to ruin him, soul and body, would consent to sell his neighbor into slavery to promote his own selfish interests, if he could do it with impunity. And if he did not rob and murder him for the sake of his money, it certainly would not be because the love of God or of man restrained him. If the love of self is so strong, that he will consent to do his neighbor the direct injury of selling him ardent spirits nothing but selfishness under some other form prevailing over the love of money, could prevent his selling men into slavery, robbing, or murdering them, to get their money. He might love his own reputation; he might fear the penalty of human law; he might fear the destruction of his own soul, so much as to restrain him from these acts of outrage and violence. But certainly it could not be the principle of love to God or man that would restrain him.

5. The individual who will enslave his fellow men for his own selfish objects, would enslave others, any or all, if his interest demanded, and if he had the same opportunity.

If a man will appropriate the rights of one, he would without any reluctance appropriate the rights of all men, if he could do it with impunity. The individual who will deprive a black man of his liberty, and enslave him, would make no scruple to enslave a white man if circumstances were equally favorable. The man who contends that the black laborer of the south ought to be held in slavery, if he dared, would contend to have the white laborers of the north enslaved, and would urge the same kind of arguments that the peace and order of society requires it, and laborers are so much better off when they have a master to take care of them. The famous Bible argument too, is as good in favor of white slaves as black, if you only had the *power* to carry it out. The man who *holds* his fellow man as property, would *take* his fellow man as property, if he could with impunity. The principle is the same in all. It is not principle that keeps men who hold slaves from kidnapping on the coast of Africa, or from making war to enslave the free laborers of the north.

6. The man that will not practice self-denial in little things to promote religion, would not endure persecution for the sake of promoting religion.

Those who will not deny their appetite would not endure the scourge and the stake. Perhaps, if persecution were to arise, some might endure it for the sake of the applause it would bring, or to show their spirit, and to face opposition. There is a natural spirit of obstinacy, which is often roused by opposition, that would go to the stake rather than yield a point. But it is easily seen, that it is not true love to the cause which prompts a man to endure opposition, if he will not endure self-denial in little things for the sake of the cause.

7. Little circumstances often discover the state of the heart.

The individual that we find delinquent in small matters, we of course infer would be much more so in larger affairs, if circumstances were equally favorable.

Where you find persons wearing little ornaments from vanity, set them down as rotten at heart. If they could they would go all lengths in display, if they were not restrained by some other considerations than a regard to the authority of God and the honor of religion. You may see this every day in the streets. Men walking with their cloaks very carefully thrown over their shoulders, so as to show the velvet; and women with their feathers tossing in the air: it is astonishing how many ways there are in which these little things show their pride and rottenness of heart.

You say these are little things. I know they are little things, and because they are little things, I mention them. It is because they are little things, that they show the character so clearly. If their pride were not deeply rooted, they would not show it in little things. If a man had it put into his power to live in a palace, with everything corresponding, it would be no wonder if he should give way to the temptation. But when his vanity shows itself in little things he gives full evidence that it has possession of his soul.

How important it is for you to see this, and to keep a watch over these little things, so as to see what you are, and to know your characters, as they appear in the sight of God.

How important to cultivate the strictest integrity, such as will carry itself out in small things as well as in large. There is something so beautiful, when you see an individual acting in little things with the same careful and conscientious uprightness as in matters of the greatest moment. Until professors of religion will cultivate this universal honesty, they will always be a reproach to religion.

Oh, how much would be gained if professors of religion would evince that entire purity and honesty on all occasions and to all persons, and do what is just right, so as to commend religion to the ungodly. How often do sinners fix their eye on some petty delinquencies of professors of religion, and look with amazement at such things in persons who profess the fear of God. What an everlasting reproach to religion, that so many of its professors are guilty of these little, mean, paltry knaveries. The wicked have cause enough to see that such professors cannot have any principle of honesty, and that such religion as they exhibit is good for nothing, and is not worth having.

Of what use is it for that woman to talk to her impenitent servant about religion, when her servant knows that she will not hesitate to overreach, and screw down, and cheat, in petty things? Or for that merchant to talk to his clerks, who know that, however honorable he may be in his greater and more public transactions, he is mean and knavish in little things? It is worse than useless.

4

LAW AND THE GOSPEL

"What shall we say then? That the Gentiles, which followed not after righteousness, have attained to righteousness, even the righteousness which is of faith. But Israel, which followed after the law of righteousness, hath not attained to the law of righteousness. Wherefore? Because they sought it not by faith, but as it were by the works of the law. For they stumbled at that stumblingstone; as it is written, Behold, I lay in Zion a stumblingstone and rock of offense: and whosoever believeth on him shall not be ashamed."
—Romans 9:30-33.

IN the Epistle to the Romans, the apostle pursues a systematic course of reasoning, to accomplish a particular design. In the beginning of it, he proves that not only the Gentiles, but the Jews also, were in a state of entire depravity; and that the Jews were not, as they vainly imagined, naturally holy. He then introduces the Moral Law, and by explaining it, shows that by works of law no flesh could be saved. His next topic is Justification by Faith, in opposition to Justification by Law. Here I will observe, in passing, that it is my design to make this the subject of my next lecture. The next subject, with which he begins chap. vi., is to show that sanctification is by faith; or that all true religion, all the acceptable obedience there ever was in the world, is based on faith. In the eighth and ninth chapters, he introduces the subject of divine sovereignty; and in the last part of the ninth chapter, he sums up the whole matter, and asks, "What shall we say then?" What shall we say of all this?—That the Gentiles who never thought of the law, have become pious, and obtained the holiness which is by faith; but the Jews attempting it by the law, have entirely failed. Wherefore? Because they made the fatal mistake of attempting to become pious by obeying the law, and have always come short, while the Gentiles have obtained true religion, by faith in Jesus Christ. Jesus Christ is here called "that stumbling-stone," because the Jews were so opposed to him. But whosoever believeth in him shall not be confounded.

My design to-night is, to point out as distinctly as I can, the true distinction between the religion of law and the religion of faith. I shall proceed in the following order ;

I. Show in what the distinction does not consist.

II. Show in what it does consist.

III. Bring forward some specimens of both, to show more plainly in what they differ.

I. I am to show in what the distinction between the religion of law and the religion of faith does not consist.

1. The difference does not lie in the fact, that under the law men were justified by works, without faith. The method of salvation in both dispensations has been the same. Sinners were always justified by faith. The Jewish dispensation pointed to a Saviour to come, and if men were saved at all, it was by faith in Christ. And sinners now are saved in the same way.

2. Not in the fact that the gospel has cancelled or set aside the obligations of the moral law. It is true, it has set aside the claims of the ceremonial law, or law of Moses. The ceremonial law was nothing but a set of types pointing to the Saviour, and was set aside, of course, when the great anti-type appeared. It is now generally admitted by all believers, that the gospel has not set aside the moral law. But that doctrine has been maintained in different ages of the church. Many have maintained that the gospel has set aside the moral law, so that believers are under no obligation to obey it. Such was the doctrine of the Nicolaitans, so severely reprobated by Christ. The An-

tinomians, in the days of the apostles and since, believed that they were without any obligation to obey the moral law; and held that Christ's righteousness was so imputed to believers, and that he had so fulfilled the law for them that they were under no obligation to obey it themselves,

There have been many, in modern times, called Perfectionists, who held that they were not under obligation to obey the law. They suppose that Christ has delivered them from the law, and given them the Spirit, and that the leadings of the Spirit are now to be their rule of life, instead of the law of God. Where the Bible says, sin shall not have dominion over believers, these persons understand by it, that the same acts, which would be sin if done by an unconverted person, are not sin in them. The others, they say, are under the law, and so bound by its rules, but themselves are sanctified, and are in Christ, and if they break the law it is no sin. But all such notions must be radically wrong. God has no right to give up the moral law. He cannot discharge us from the duty of love to God and love to man, for this is right in itself. And unless God will alter the whole moral constitution of the universe, so as to make that right which is wrong, he cannot give up the claims of the moral law. Besides, this doctrine represents Jesus Christ and the Holy Ghost as having taken up arms openly against the government of God.

3. The distinction between law religion and gospel religion does not consist in the fact that the gospel is any less strict in its claims, or allows any greater latitude of self-indulgence than the law. Not only does the gospel not cancel the' obligations of the moral law, but it does in no degree abate them. Some people talk about gospel liberty; as though they had got a new rule of life, less strict, and allowing more liberty than the law. I admit that it has provided a new method of justification, but it every where insists that the rule of life is the same with

the law. The very first sentence of the gospel, the command to repent, is in effect a re-enactment of the law, for it is a command to return to obedience. The idea that the liberty of the gospel differs from the liberty of the law is erroneous.

4. Neither does the distinction consist in the fact that those called legalists, or who have a legal religion, do, either by profession or in fact, depend on their own works for justification. It is not often the case, at least in our day, that legalists do profess dependence on their own works, for there are few so ignorant as not to know that this is directly in the face of the gospel. Nor is it necessarily the case that they really depend on their own works. Often they really depend on Christ for salvation. But their dependence is false dependence, such as they have no right to have. They depend on him, but they make it manifest that their faith, or dependence, is not that which actually " worketh by love, " or that " purifieth the heart, ' or that " overcometh the world." It is a simple matter of fact that the faith which they have does not do what the faith does which men must have in order to be saved, and so it is not the faith of the gospel. They have a kind of faith, but not that kind that makes men real Christians, and brings them under the terms of the gospel.

II. I am to mention some of the particulars in which these two kinds of religion differ.

There are several different classes of persons who manifestly have a legal religion. There are some who really profess to depend on their own works for salvation. Such were the pharisees. The Hicksite Quakers formerly took this ground, and maintained that men were to be justified by works ; setting aside entirely justification by faith. When I speak of works, I mean works of law. And here I want you to distinguish between works of law and works of faith. This is the grand distinction to be kept in view

It is between works produced by legal considerations, and those produced by faith. There are but two principles on which obedience to any government can turn : One is the principle of hope and fear, under the influence of conscience. Conscience points out what is right or wrong, and the individual is induced by hope and fear to obey. The other principle is confidence and love. You see this illustrated in families, where one child always obeys from hope and fear, and another from affectionate confidence. So in the government of God, the only thing that ever produces even the appearance of obedience, is one of these two principles.

There is a multitude of things that address our hopes and fears ; such as character, interest, heaven, and hell, etc. These may produce external obedience, or conformity to the law. But filial confidence leads men to obey God from love. This is the only obedience that is acceptable to God. God not only requires a certain course of conduct, but that this should spring from love. There never was and never can be, in the government of God, any acceptable obedience but the obedience of faith. Some suppose that faith will be done away in heaven. This is a strange notion. As if there were no occasion to trust God in heaven, or no reason to exercise confidence in him. Here is the great distinction between the religion of law and gospel religion. Legal obedience is influenced by hope and fear, and is hypocritical, selfish, outward, constrained. Gospel obedience is from love, and is sincere, free, cheerful, true. There is a class of legalists, who depend on works of law for justification, who have merely deified what they call a principle of right, and have set themselves to do right ; it is not out of respect to the law of God, or out of love to God, but just because it is right.

There is another distinction here. The religion of law is the religion of purposes, or desires, founded on legal considerations, and not the religion of preference, or love to God. The individual intends to put off his sins; he purposes to obey God and be religious; but his purpose does not grow out of love to God, but out of hope and fear. It is easy to see that a purpose, founded on such considerations, is very different from a purpose growing out of love. But the religion of the gospel is not a purpose merely, but an actual preference consisting in love.

Again, there is a class of legalists that depend on Christ, but their dependence is not gospel dependence, because the works which it produces are works of law; that is, from hope and fear, not from love. Gospel dependence may produce, perhaps, the very same outward works, but the motives are radically different. The legalist drags on a painful, irksome, moral, and perhaps, outwardly, religious life. The gospel believer has an affectionate confidence in God, which leads him to obey out of love. His obedience is prompted by his own feelings. Instead of being dragged to duty, he goes to it cheerfully, because he loves it, and doing it is a delight to his soul.

There is another point. The legalist expects to be justified by faith, but he has not learned that he must be sanctified by faith. I propose to examine this point another time, in full. Modern legalists do not expect to be justified by works; they know these are inadequate—they know that the way to be saved is by Christ. But they have no practical belief that justification by faith is only true, as sanctification by faith is true, and that men are justified by faith only, as they are first sanctified by faith. And therefore, while they expect to be justified by faith, they set themselves to perform works that are works of law.

Again: I wish you to observe that the two classes may agree in these points; the necessity of good works, and, theoretically, in what constitutes good works; that is, obedience springing from love to God. And further, they may agree in aiming to perform good works of this kind. But the difference lies here—in the different influences to which they look, to enable them to perform good works. The considerations by which they expect their minds to be affected, are different. They look to different sources for motives. And the true Christian alone succeeds in actually performing good works. The legalist, aiming to perform good works, influenced by hope and fear, and a selfish regard to his own interest, obeying the voice of conscience because he is afraid to do otherwise, falls entirely short of loving God with all his heart, and soul, and strength. The motives under which he acts have no tendency to bring him to the obedience of love. The true Christian, on the contrary, so appreciates God, so perceives and understands God's character, in Christ, as begets such an affectionate confidence in God, that he finds it easy to obey from love. Instead of finding it, as a hymn has strangely represented,

"Hard to obey, and harder still to love,"

he finds it no hardship at all. The commandments are not grievous. The yoke is easy, and the burden light. And he finds the ways of wisdom to be ways of pleasantness, and all her paths to be peace.

Is it so with most professors of religion? Is it so with *you?* Do you feel, in your religious duties constrained by love? Are you drawn by such strong cords of love, that it would give you more trouble to omit duty than to obey? Do your affections flow out in such a strong current to God, that you cannot but obey? How is it with those individuals who find it "hard to obey, and harder still to love?" What is the matter? Ask that wife who loves her husband, if she finds it hard to try to please her husband! Suppose she answers, in a solemn tone, "O yes, I find it hard to obey and harder still to love my husband," what would the husband think ? What would any one of you who are parents say, if you should hear one of your children complaining, "I find it harder to obey my father, and harder still to love ?" The truth is, there is a radical defect in the religion of those people who love such expressions and live as if they were true. If any one of you find religion a painful thing, rely on it, you have the religion of the law. Did you ever find it a painful thing to do what you love to do ? No. It is a pleasure to do it. The religion of the gospel is no labor to them that exercise it. It is the feeling of the heart. What would you do in heaven, if religion is such a painful thing here ?—Suppose you were taken to heaven and obliged to grind out just so much religion every week, and month and year, to eternity. What sort of a heaven would it be to you ? Would it be heaven, or would it be hell ?—If you were required to have ten thousand times as much as you have here, and your whole life were to be filled up with this, and nothing else to do or enjoy but an eternal round of such duties, would not hell itself be a respite to you ?

The difference, then, lies here. One class are striving to be religious from hope and fear, and under the influence of conscience which lashes them if they do not do their duty. The other class act from love to God, and the impulses of their own feelings, and know what the text means, which says, "I will put my law in their inward parts, and write it on their hearts, I will be their God, and they shall be my people."

III. I will give some specimens of these two classes, by way of illustration.

The first example I shall give is that of the apostle Paul, as he has recorded it in the 7th of Romans, where he exhibits the struggle to obey the law, under the influence of law alone. [Here Mr. Finney proceeded, at a considerable length, to comment on the 7th chapter of Romans, but as he has since concluded to give a separate lecture on that subject, these remarks are omitted here. He showed how Paul had struggled, and labored, under the motives of law, until he absolutely despaired of help from that quarter; and how, when the gospel was brought to view, the chain was broken, and he found it easy to obey. He then proceeded.]

You may see the same in the experience of almost any convicted sinner, after he has become truly converted. He was convicted, the law was brought home to his mind, he struggled to fulfil the law, he was in agony, and then he was filled with joy and glory. Why? He was agonized under the law, he had no rest and no satisfaction, he tried to please God by keeping the law, he went about in pain all the day, he read the Bible, he tried to pray; but the Spirit of God was upon him, showing him his sins, and he had no relief. The more he attempts to help himself the deeper he sinks in despair. All the while his heart is cold and selfish. But now let another principle be introduced, and let him be influenced by love to God. The same Holy Spirit is upon him, showing him the same sins that grieved and distressed him so before. But now he goes on his knees, his tears flow like water as he confesses his guilt, and his heart melts in joyful relentings, such as cannot be described, but easily understood by them that have felt it. Now he engages in performing the same duties that he tried before. But, O, how changed! The Spirit of God has broken his chains, and now he loves God and is filled with joy aud peace in believing.

The same thing is seen in many professors of religion, who find religion a painful thing. They have much conviction, and perhaps much of what they call religion, but their minds are chiefly filled with doubts and fears, doubts and fears all the time. By and by, perhaps, that same professor will come out, all at once, a different character. His religion now is not all complaints and sighs, but the love of God fills his heart, and he goes cheerfully and happily to his duty ; and his soul is so light and happy in God, that he floats in an ocean of love and joy, and the peace that fills him is like a river.

Here, then, is the difference between the slavery of law and the liberty of the gospel. The liberty of the gospel does not consist in being freed from doing what the law requires, but in a man's being in such a state of mind that doing it is itself a pleasure instead of a burden. What is the difference between slavery and freedom ? The slave serves because he is obliged to do so, the freeman serves from choice. The man who is under the bondage of law does duty because conscience thunders in his ears if he does not obey, and he hopes to go to heaven if he does. The man who is in the liberty of the gospel does the same things because he loves to do them. One is influenced by selfishness, the other by disinterested benevolence.

CONCLUSION

I. You can easily see, that if we believe the words and actions of most professors of religion, they have made a mistake ; and that they have the religion of law, and not gospel religion. They are not constrained by the love of Christ, but moved by hopes and fears, and by the commandments of God. They have gone no farther in religion than to be convicted sinners. Within the last year, I have witnessed the regeneration of so many professors of religion, that I am led to fear that great multitudes in the church are yet under the law ; and although they profess to depend on Christ for salvation, their faith is not that which works by love.

II. Some persons are all faith without works. These are Antinomians. Others are all works and no faith :

these are legalists. In all ages of the church, men have inclined first to one of these extremes, and then over to the other. Sometimes they are settled down on their lees, pretending to be all faith, and waiting God's time; then they get roused up, and dash on in works, without regard to the motive from which they act.

III. You see the true character of those professors of religion who are for ever crying out "Legality!" as soon as they are pressed up to holiness. When I first began to preach, I found this spirit in many places; so that the moment Christians were urged up to duty, the cry would rise, This is legal preaching—do preach the gospel; salvation is by faith, not by duty; you ought to comfort saints, not distress them. All this was nothing but rank Antinomianism.

On the other hand, the same class of churches now complain, if you preach faith to them, and show them what is the true nature of gospel faith. They now want to do something, and insist that no preaching is good that does not excite them, and stir them up to good works. They are all for doing, doing, doing, and will be dissatisfied with preaching that discriminates between true and false faith, and urges obedience of the heart, out of love to God. The Antinomians wait for God to produce right feelings in them. The Legalists undertake to get right feelings by going to work. It is true that going to work is the way, when the church feels right, to perpetuate and cherish right feelings. But it is not the way to get right feeling, in the first place, to dash right into the work, without any regard to the motives of the heart.

IV. Real Christians are a stumbling-block to both parties; to those who wait God's time and do nothing, and to those who bustle about with no faith. The true Christian acts under such a love to God and to his fellow man, and he labors to pull sinners out of the fire with such earnestness, that the waiting party cry out, "Oh, he is getting up an excitement; he is going to work in his own strength; he does not believe in the necessity of divine influences; we ought to feel our dependence; let us wait God's time, and not try to get up a revival without God." So they sit down and fold their hands, and sing, "We feel our dependence, we feel our dependence; wait God's time; we do not trust in our own works." On the other hand, the legalists, when once they get roused to bustle about, will not see but their religion is the same with the real Christian's. They make as strenuous outward efforts, and suppose themselves to be actuated by the same spirit.

You will rarely see a revival, in which this does not show itself. If the body of the church are awakened to duty, and have the spirit of prayer and zeal for the conversion of sinners, there will be some who sit still and complain that the church are depending on their own strength, and others very busy and noisy, but without any feeling while the third class are so full of love and compassion to sinners that they can hardly eat or sleep, and yet so humble and tender that you would imagine they felt themselves to be nothing. The legalist, with his dry zeal, makes a great noise, deceives himself, perhaps, and thinks he is acting just like a Christian. But mark! The true Christian is stirring and active in the service of Christ, but moves with the holy fire that burns within his bosom. The legalist depends on some protracted meeting, or some other influence from without, to excite him to do his duty.

V. You see why the religion of some persons is so steady and uniform, and that of others, is so fitful and evanescent. You will find some individuals, who seem to be always engaged in religion. Talk to them any time, on the subject, and their souls will kindle. Others are awake only now and then. Once in a while you may find them full of zeal. The truth is, when one has the anointing that abides, he has something that is durable. But if his religion is only that of the law, he will only have just so much of it as he has of conviction at the present moment, and his religion will be fitful and evanescent, of course.

VI. You see why some are so anxious to get to heaven, while others are so happy here. There are some, who have such a love for souls, and such a desire to have Christ's kingdom built upon earth, that they are perfectly happy here, and willing to live and labor for God, as long as he chooses to have them. Nay, if they were sent to hell, and permitted to labor there for souls, they would be happy. While others talk as if people were never to expect true enjoyment in this life ; but when they get to heaven, they expect to be happy. One class have no enjoyment but in hope. The other has already the reality, the very substance of heaven begun in the soul.

Now, beloved, I have as particularly as I could in the time, pointed out to you the distinction between the religion of the law and the religion of the gospel. And now, what religion have you ? True religion is always the same, and consists in disinterested love to God and man. Have you that kind of religion ? Or have you the kind that consists, not in disinterested love, but in the pursuit of happiness as the great end. Which have you ? The fruits of the Spirit are love, joy, peace. There is no condemnation of such religion. But if any man have not the spirit of Christ, he is none of his. Now, don't make a mistake here, and suffer yourselves to go down to hell with a lie in your right hand, because you have the religion of the law. The Jews failed here, while the Gentiles attained true holiness by the gospel. O, how many are deceived, and are acting under legal considerations, while they know nothing of the real religion of the gospel !

5

SANCTIFICATION BY FAITH

"Do we then make void the law through faith? God forbid: yea, we establish the law." —Romans 3:31

THE apostle had been proving that all mankind, both Jews and Gentiles, were in their sins, and refuting the doctrine so generally entertained by the Jews, that they were a holy people and saved by their works. He showed that justification can never be by works, but by faith. He then anticipates an objection, like this, "Are we to understand you as teaching that the law of God is abrogated and set aside by this plan of justification?" "By no means," says the apostle, "we rather establish the law." In treating of this subject, I design to pursue the following order :

I. Show that the gospel method of justification does not set aside or repeal the law.

II. That it rather establishes the law, by producing true obedience to it, and as the only means that does this.

The greatest objection to the doctrine of Justification by Faith has always been, that it is inconsistent with good morals, conniving at sin, and opening the flood-gates of iniquity. It has been said, that to maintain that men are not to depend on their own good behavior for salvation, but are to be saved by faith in another, is calculated to make men regardless of good morals, and to encourage them to live in sin, depending on Christ to justify them. By others, it has been maintained that the gospel does in fact release from obligation to obey the moral law, so that a more lax morality is permitted under the gospel than was allowed under the law.

I. I am to show that the gospel method of justification does not set aside the moral law.

1. It cannot be that this method of justification sets aside the moral law, because the gospel everywhere enforces obedience to the law, and lays down the same standard of holiness.

Jesus Christ adopted the very words of the moral law, "Thou shalt love the Lord thy God with all thy heart, and with all thy soul, and with all thy mind, and with all thy strength, and thy neighbor as thyself."

2. The conditions of the gospel are designed to sustain the moral law.

The gospel requires repentance as the condition of salvation. What is repentance? The renunciation of sin. The man must repent of his breaches of the law of God, and return to obedience to the law. This is tantamount to a requirement of obedience.

3. The gospel maintains that the law is right.

If it did not maintain the law to its full extent, it might be said that Christ is the minister of sin.

4. By the gospel plan, the sanctions of the gospel are added to the sanctions of the law, to enforce obedience to the law.

The apostle says, "He that despised Moses' law, died without mercy under two or three witnesses; of how much sorer punishment, suppose ye, shall he be thought worthy, who hath trodden under foot the Son of God, and hath counted the blood of the covenant, wherewith he was sanctified, an unholy thing, and hath done despite unto the spirit of grace?" Thus adding the awful sanctions of the gospel to those of the law, to enforce obedience to the precepts of the law.

II. I am to show that the doctrine of justification by faith produces sanctification, by producing the only true obedience to the law.

By this I mean, that when the mind understands this plan, and exercises faith in it, it naturally produces sanctification. Sanctification is holiness, and holiness is nothing but obedience to the law, consisting in love to God and love to man.

In support of the proposition that justification by faith produces true obedience to the law of God, my first position is, that sanctification never can be produced among selfish or wicked beings, by the law itself, separate from the considerations of the gospel, or the motives connected with justification by faith.

The motives of the law did not restrain those beings from committing sin, and it is absurd to suppose the same motives can "reclaim" them from sin, when they have fallen under the power of selfishness, and when sin is a confirmed habit. The motives of the law lose a part of their influence, when a being is once fallen. They even exert an opposite influence. The motives of the law, as viewed by a selfish mind, have a tendency to cause sin to abound. This is the experience of every sinner. When he sees the spirituality of the law, and does not see the motives of the gospel, it raises the pride of his heart, and hardens him in his rebellion. The case of the devil is an exhibition of what the law can do, with all its principles and sanctions, upon a wicked heart. He understands the law, sees its reasonableness, has experienced the blessedness of obedience, and knows full well that to return to obedience would restore his peace of mind. This he knows better than any sinner of our race, who never was holy, can know it, and yet it presents to his mind no such motives as reclaim him, but on the contrary, drive him to a returnless distance from obedience.

When obedience to the law is held forth to the sinner as the condition of life, immediately it sets him upon making self-righteous efforts. In almost every instance, the first effort of the awakened sinner is to obey the **law.** He thinks he must first make himself better, in some **way,** before he may embrace the gospel. He has no idea of **the** simplicity of the gospel plan of salvation by faith, offering eternal life as a mere gratuitous gift. Alarm the sinner with the penalty of the law, and he naturally, and by the very laws of his mind, sets himself to do better, to amend his life, and in some self-righteous manner obtain eternal life, under the influence of slavish fear. And the more the law presses him, the greater are his pharisaical efforts, while hope is left to him, that if he obeys he may be accepted. What else could you expect of him ? He is purely selfish, and though he ought to submit at once to God, yet, as he does not understand the gospel terms of salvation, and his mind is of course first turned to the object of getting away from the danger of the penalty, he tries to get up to heaven some other way. I do not believe there is an instance in history, of a man who has submitted to God, until he has seen that salvation must be by faith, and that his own self-righteous strivings have no tendency to save him.

Again ; if you undertake to produce holiness by legal motives, the very fear of failure has the effect to divert attention from the objects of love, from God and Christ. The sinner is all the while compassing Mount Sinai, and taking heed to his footsteps, to see how near he comes to obedience ; and how can he get into the spirit of heaven ?

Again ; the penalty of the law has no tendency to produce love in the first instance. It may increase love in those who already have it, when they contemplate it as an exhibition of God's infinite holiness. The angels in heaven, and good men on earth, contemplate its propriety and fitness, and see in it the expression of the good will of God to his creatures, and it appears amiable and lovely, and increases their delight in God and their confidence towards him. But it is right the reverse with the selfish man. He sees the penalty hanging over his own head, and no way of escape, and it is not in mind to become enamored with the Being that holds the thunderbolt over his devoted head. From the nature of mind, he will flee from him, not to him. It seems never to have been dreamed of, by the inspired writers, that the law could sanctify men. The law is given rather to slay than to make alive, to cut off men's self-righteous hopes for ever, and compel them to flee to Christ.

Again ; Sinners, under the naked law, and irrespective of the gospel—I say, sinners, naturally and necessarily, and of right, under such circumstances, view God as an irreconcilable enemy. They are wholly selfish ; and apart from the considerations of the gospel, they view God just as the devil views him. No motive in the law can be exhibited to a selfish mind that will beget love. Can the influence of penalty do it ?

A strange plan of reformation this, to send men to hell to reform them ! Let them go on in sin and rebellion to the end of life, and then be punished until he becomes holy. I wonder the devil has not become holy ! He has suffered long enough, he has been in hell these thousands of years, and he is no better than he was. The reason is, there is no gospel there, and no Holy Spirit to apply the truth, and the penalty only confirms his rebellion.

Again : The doctrine of justification can relieve these difficulties. It can produce, and has produced, real obedience to the precept of the law. Justification by faith does not set aside the law as a rule of duty, but only sets aside the penalty of the law. And the preaching of justification as a mere gratuity, bestowed on the simple act of faith, is the only way in which obedience to the law is ever brought about. This I shall now show from the following considerations :

1. It relieves the mind from the pressure of those considerations that naturally tend to confirm selfishness.

While the mind is looking only at the law, it only feels the influence of hope and fear, perpetuating purely selfish efforts. But justification by faith annihilates this spirit of bondage. The apostle says, "We have not received the spirit of bondage again to fear." This plan of salvation begets love and gratitude to God, and leads the souls to taste the sweets of holiness.

2. It relieves the mind also from the necessity of making its own salvation its supreme object.

The believer in the gospel plan of salvation finds salvation, full and complete, including both sanctification and eternal life, already prepared ; and instead of being driven to the life of a Pharisee in religion, of laborious and exhausting effort, he receives it as a free gift, a mere gratuity, and is now left free to exercise disinterested benevolence, and to live and labor for the salvation of others, leaving his own soul unreservedly to Christ.

3. The fact that God has provided and given him salvation as a gratuity, is calculated to awaken in the believer a concern for others, when he sees them dying for the want of this salvation, that they may be brought to the knowledge of the truth and be saved. How far from every selfish motive are those influences. It exhibits God, not as the law exhibits him, as an irreconcilable enemy, but as a grieved and offended Father, willing to be reconciled, nay, very desirous that his subjects should become reconciled, to him and live. This is calculated to beget love. It exhibits God as making the greatest sacrifice to reconcile sinners to himself ; and from no other motive than a pure and disinterested regard to their happiness. Try this in your own family. The law represents God as armed with wrath, and determined to punish the sinner, without hope or help. The gospel represents him as offended, indeed, but yet so

anxious they should return to him, that he has made the greatest conceivable sacrifices, out of pure disinterested love to his wandering children.

I once heard a father say, that he had tried in his family to imitate the government of God, and when his child did wrong, he reasoned with him and showed him his faults ; and when he was fully convinced and confounded and condemned, so that he had not a word to say, then the father asked him, Do you deserve to be punished ? Yes, sir. I know it, and now if I were to let you go, what influence would it have over the other children ? Rather than do that, I will take the punishment myself. So he laid the ferule on himself, and it had the most astonishing effect on the mind of the child. He had never tried anything so perfectly subduing to the mind as this. And from the laws of mind, it must be so. If affects the mind in a manner entirely different from the naked law.

4. It brings the mind under an entire new set of influences, and leaves it free to weigh the reasons for holiness, and decide accordingly.

Under the law, none but motives of hope and fear can operate on the sinner's mind. But under the gospel, the influence of hope and fear are set aside, and a new set of considerations presented, with a view of God's entire character, in all the attractions he can command. It gives the most heart-breaking, sin-subduing views of God. It presents him to the senses in human nature. It exhibits his disinterestedness. The way Satan prevailed against our first parents was by leading them to doubt God's disinterestedness. The gospel demonstrates the truth, and corrects this lie. The law represents God as the inexorable enemy of the sinner, as securing happiness to all who perfectly obey, but thundering down wrath on all who disobey. The gospel reveals new features in God's character, not known before. Doubtless the gospel increases the love of all holy beings, and gives greater joy to the angels in heaven, greatly increasing their love, and confidence, and admiration, when they see God's amazing pity and forbearance towards the guilty. The law drove the devils to hell, and it drove Adam and Eve from Paradise. But when the blessed spirits see the same holy God waiting on rebels, nay opening his own bosom, and giving his beloved Son for them, and taking such unwearied pains for thousands of years to save sinners, do you think it has no influence in strengthening the motives in their minds to obedience and love?

The devil, who is a purely selfish being, is always accusing others of being selfish. He accused Job of this: "Doth Job fear God for nought?" He accused God to our first parents, of being selfish, and that the only reason for his forbidding them to eat of the tree of knowledge was the fear that they might come to know as much as himself. The gospel shows what God is. If he were selfish, he would not take such pains to save those whom he might, with perfect ease, crush to hell. Nothing is so calculated to make selfish persons ashamed of their selfishness, as to see disinterested benevolence in others. Hence the wicked are always trying to appear disinterested. Let the selfish individual who has any heart, see true benevolence in others, and it is like coals of fire on his head. The wise men understood this, when he said, "If thine enemy hunger, feed him; if he thirst, give him drink; for in so doing, thou shalt heap coals of fire on his head." Nothing is so calculated to cut down an enemy, and win him over, and make him a friend.

This is what the gospel does to sinners. It shows that notwithstanding all that they have done to God, God still exercises toward them disinterested love. When he sees God stooping from heaven to save him, and understands that it is indeed true, oh, how it melts and breaks down the heart, strikes a death-blow to selfishness, and wins him over to unbounded confidence and holy love. God has so constituted the mind, that it must necessarily do homage to virtue. It must do this, as long as it retains the powers of moral agency. This is as true in hell as in heaven. The devil feels this. When an individual sees that God has no interested motives to condemn him, when he sees that God offers salvation as a mere gratuity, through faith, he cannot but feel admiration of God's benevolence. His selfishness is crushed, the law has done its work, he sees that all his selfish endeavors have done no good; and the next step is for his heart to go out in disinterested love.

Suppose a man was under sentence of death for rebellion, and had tried many expedients to recommend himself to the government, but failed, because they were all hollow-hearted and selfish. He sees that the government understands his motives, and that he is not really reconciled. He knows himself that they were all hypocritical and selfish, moved by the hope of favor or the fear of wrath, and that the government is more and more incensed at his hypocrisy. Just now let a paper be brought to him from the government, offering him a free pardon on the simple condition that he would receive it as mere gratuity, making no account of his own works—what influence will it have on his mind? The moment he finds the penalty set aside, and that he has no need to go to work by any self-righteous efforts, his mind is filled with admiration. Now, let it appear that the government has made the greatest sacrifices to procure this; his selfishness is slain, and he melts down like a child at his sovereign's feet, ready to obey the law because he loves his sovereign.

5. All true obedience turns on faith. It secures all the requisite influences to produce sanctification. It gives the doctrines of eternity access to the mind and a hold on the heart. In this world the motives of time are addressed to

the senses. The motives that influence the spirits of the just in heaven do not reach us through the senses. But when faith is exercised, the wall is broken down, and the vast realities of eternity act on the mind here with the same kind of influence that they have in eternity. Mind is mind, every where. And were it not for the darkness of unbelief, men would live here just as they do in the eternal world. Sinners here would rage and blaspheme, just as they do in hell ; and saints would love and obey and praise, just as they do in heaven. Now, faith makes all these things realities, it swings the mind loose from the clogs of the world, and he beholds God, and apprehends his law and his love. In no other way *can* these motives take hold on the mind. What a mighty action must it have on the mind, when it takes hold of the love of Christ ! What a life-giving power, when the pure motives of the gospel crowd into the mind and stir it up with energy divine ! Every Christian knows, that in proportion to the strength of his faith, his mind is buoyant and active, and when his faiths flags, his soul is dark and listless. It is faith alone that places the things of time and eternity in their true comparison, and sets down the things of time and sense at their real value. It breaks up the delusions of the mind, the soul shakes itself from its errors and clogs, and it rises up in communion with God.

CONCLUSION

I. It is as unphilosophical as it is unscriptural to attempt to convert and sanctify the minds of sinners without the motives of the gospel.

You may press the sinner with the law, and make him see his own character, the greatness and justice of God, and his ruined condition. But hide the motives of the gospel from his mind, and it is all in vain.

II. It is absurd to think that the offers of the gospel are calculated to beget a selfish hope.

Some are afraid to throw out upon the sinner's mind all the character of God ; and they try to make him submit to God, by casting him down in despair.   This is not only against the gospel, but it is absurd in itself.   It is absurd to think that, in order to destroy the selfishness of a sinner, you must hide from him the knowledge of how much God loves and pities him, and how great sacrifices he has made to save him.

III. So far is it from being true that sinners are in danger of getting false hopes if they are allowed to know the real compassion of God, while you hide this, it is impossible to give him any other than a false hope.   Withholding from the sinner who is writhing under conviction, the fact that God has provided salvation as a mere gratuity, is the very way to confirm his selfishness ; and if he gets any hope, it must be a false one.   To press him to submission by the law alone, is to set him to build a self-righteous foundation.

IV. So far as we can see, salvation by grace, not bestowed in any degree for our own works, is the only possible way of reclaiming selfish beings.

Suppose salvation was not altogether gratuitous, but that some degree of good works was taken into the account, and for those good works in part we were justified— just so far as this consideration is in the mind, just so far there is a stimulus to selfishness.   You must bring the sinner to see that he is entirely dependent on free grace, and that a full and complete justification is bestowed, on the first act of faith, as a mere gratuity, and no part of it as an equivalent for any thing he is to do.   This alone dissolves the influence of selfishnesss, and secures holy action.

V. If all this is true, sinners should be put in the fullest possible possession, and in the speediest manner, of the whole plan of salvation.

They should be made to see the law, and their own guilt, and that they have no way to save themselves; and then, the more fully the whole length and breadth, and height, and depth of the love of God should be opened, the more effectually will you crush his selfishness, and subdue his soul in love to God. Do not be afraid, in conversing with sinners, to show the whole plan of salvation, and give the fullest possible exhibition of the infinite compassion of God. Show him that, notwithstanding his guilt, the Son of God is knocking at the door and beseeching him to be reconciled to God.

VI. You see why so many convicted sinners continue so long compassing Mount Sinai, with self-righteous efforts to save themselves by their own works.

How often you find sinners trying to get more feeling, or waiting till they have made more prayers and made greater efforts, and expecting to recommend themselves to God in this way. Why is all this? The sinner needs to be driven off from this, and made to see that he is all the while looking for salvation under the law. He must be made to see that all this is superseded by the gospel offering him all he wants as a mere gratuity. He must hear Jesus saying, " Ye will not come *unto me* that ye may have life: O, no, you are willing to pray, and go to meeting, and read the Bible, or any thing, but come unto me. Sinner, this is the road; I am the way, and the truth, and the life. No man cometh to the Father but by me. I am the resurrection and the life. I am the light of the world. Here, sinner, is what you want. Instead of trying your self-righteous prayers and efforts, here is what you are looking for, only believe and you shall be saved."

VII. You see why so many professors of religion are always in the dark.

They are looking at their sins, confining their observations to themselves, and losing sight of the fact, that they have only to take right hold of Jesus Christ, and throw themselves upon him, and all is well.

VIII. The law is useful to convict men; but, as a matter of fact, it never breaks the heart. The Gospel alone does that. The degree in which a convert is broken hearted, is in proportion to the degree of clearness with which he apprehends the gospel.

IX. Converts, if you call them so, who entertain a hope under legal preaching, may have an intellectual approbation of the law, and a sort of dry zeal, but never make mellow, broken hearted Christians. If they have not seen God in the attitude in which he is exhibited in the gospel, they are not such Christians as you will see sometimes, with the tear trembling in their eye, and their frames shaking with emotion, at the name of Jesus.

X. Sinners under conviction, and professors in darkness, must be led right to Christ, and made to take hold of the plan of salvation by faith. You cannot do them good in any other way.

6

NECESSITY OF DIVINE TEACHING

"Nevertheless I tell you the truth; it is expedient for you that I go away: for if I go not away, the Comforter will not come unto you; but if I depart, I will send him unto you. And when he is come, he will reprove the world of sin, and of righteousness, and of judgment: of sin, because they believe not on me; of righteousness, because I go to my Father, and ye see me no more; of judgment, because the prince of this world is judged. I have yet many things to say unto you, but ye cannot bear them now. Howbeit when he, the Spirit of truth, is come, he will guide you into all truth: for he shall not speak of himself; but whatsoever he shall hear, that shall he speak: and he will show you things to come." —John 16:7-13.

THE doctrine of the necessity of Divine Influence, to enlighten and sanctify the minds of men, is very abundantly taught in the Bible, and is generally maintained, as a matter of opinion at least, in all orthodox churches. But, as a matter of fact, there seems to be very little available knowledge of the gospel among mankind ; so little that it exerts comparatively little influence. The great ends of the gospel have hardly begun to be realized, in the production of holiness on the earth. It is a grand question, whether we do need Divine Influence to attain the ends of the gospel ; and if we do need it, then in what degree do we need it, and why ? If our minds are unsettled on this question, we shall be unsettled on all the subjects that practically concern our sanctification.

In discoursing on this subject to-night, I design to pursue the following order :

I. Inquire how far the reason of man, unaided by Divine illumination, is capable of understanding the things of religion.

II. Show wherein the reason of man is defective, in regard to the capacity of gaining any available knowledge of the gospel.

III. That the Spirit of God alone can supply the illumination that is needed.

IV. That every one may have the influence of the Spirit, according to his necessities.

V. The reasons why any individual fails to receive this divine aid to the extent of his necessities.

VI. That men are responsible for the light which they might have, as well as for that which they actually enjoy.

I. I shall inquire how far the reason of man, unaided by Divine illumination, is capable of apprehending the things of religion.

1. The mind of man is capable of understanding the historical facts of religion, just as it comprehends any other historical facts.

2. It is capable of understanding the doctrinal propositions of the gospel.

That is, it can understand those abstractions which make up the skeleton of the gospel ; such as the being and character of God, the divine authority and inspiration of the scriptures, and other fundamental doctrines which make up the frame-work of the gospel. That is, it can understand them as propositions, and see the evidence that supports them as true, just as it can understand any propositions in science.

For instance, to enter a little into detail—A man, by his reason, may understand the law of God. He can understand that it requires him to exercise perfect love towards God and all other beings. He can see the ground of his obligation to do this, because he is a moral being. He knows, by experience, what love is, for he has exercised love towards different objects. And he can, therefore, form or comprehend the idea of love, so far as to see the reasonableness of the requirement. He can understand the foundation and the force of moral obligation, and see, in some measure, the extent of his obligation to love God.

So, likewise, he can see that he is a sinner, and that he cannot be saved by his own works. He has broken the law, so that the law can never justify him. He can see, that if he is ever saved, he must be justified through mere mercy, by an act of pardon.

I might go through the whole circle of theology, and show that the human understanding is capable of knowing it, in the abstract, as a system of propositions, to be received and believed, on evidence, like any other science. I do not mean to be understood as saying, that unaided reason can attain any available knowledge of the things of religion, or any such knowledge as will be effectual to produce a sanctifying change.

II. I am to show wherein our knowledge of the things of religion is necessarily defective, without the aids of the Holy Spirit.

In other words, I am to show what our knowledge of the gospel lacks, to make it available to salvation.

And here it is necessary to distinguish between knowledge which might be available to one that was himself disposed to love and obey God ; and what will be available, in fact, to a sinner, who is wholly indisposed to holiness. It is easy to see that one who is disposed to do right would be influenced to duty by a far less amount of illumination, or a far less clear and vivid view of motives, than one who is disposed to do wrong. What we are now inquiring after respects the matter of fact, in this world. Whether the knowledge attainable by our present faculties would be available to influence us to do right, were there no sin in the world, is more than I can say. As a matter of fact, the knowledge which Adam had when in a state of innocency did not avail to influence him to do right. But we are now speaking of things as they are in this world, and to show what is the reason that men, as sinners, can have no available knowledge of divine things ; no such knowledge as will, as a matter of fact, influence them to love and serve God.

Knowledge, to avail anything towards effecting its object, must be such as will influence the mind. The will must be controlled. And to do this, the mind must have such a view of things as to excite emotion, corresponding to the object in view. Mere intellect never will move the soul to act. A pure scientific abstraction of the intellect, that does not touch the feelings, or excite any emotion, is wholly unavailable to move the will. It is so every where. It would be so in heaven. You must bring the mind under a degree of excitement, to influence the will in any case. In the case of sinners, to influence sinners to love God, you must have a great degree of light, such as will powerfully excite the mind, and produce strong emotions. The reasons for obedience must be made to appear with great strength and vividness, so as to subdue their rebellious hearts and bring them voluntarily to obey God. This is available knowledge. This men never have, and never can have, without the Spirit of God. If men were disposed to do right, I know not how far their knowledge, attainable by unaided reason, might avail. But, as they are universally and totally indisposed, this knowledge will never do it. I will mention some of the reasons :

1. All the knowledge we can have here of spiritual things, is by analogy, or comparison.

Our minds are here shut up in the body, and we derive all our ideas from external objects, through the senses. Now, we never can of ourselves obtain knowledge of spiritual or eternal things in this way sufficient to rightly influence our wills. Our bodily powers were not created for this. All the ideas we can have of the spiritual world is by analogy, or comparing them with the things around us. It is easily seen that all ideas conveyed to our minds in this way, must be extremely imperfect, and that we do not,

after all, get the true idea in our minds. The Jewish
types were probably the most forcible means which God
could then use, for giving to the Jews a correct idea of the
gospel. Considering how the eastern nations were accustomed, by their education, to the use of figures, and para-
bles, and types, probably the system of types was the most
impressive and happy mode that could be devised to gain
a more ready access for the truth to their minds, and give
them a more full idea of the plan of redemption than could
be communicated in any other way. And yet it is manifest that the ideas which were communicated in this way
were extremely imperfect; and that, without divine illumination to make them see the reality more fully than they
could by unaided reason, they never would have got any
available knowledge in this way.

So words are merely signs of ideas. They are not the
ideas, but the representatives of ideas. It is often very
difficult, and sometimes impossible to convey ideas by
words. Take a little child, and attempt to talk with him,
and how difficult it is, on many subjects, to get your ideas
into his little mind. He must have some experience of the
things you are trying to teach, before you can convey ideas
to him by words.

Suppose this congregation were all blind, and had never
seen colors. Then suppose that on that wall hung a most
grand and beautiful painting, and that I was a perfect
master of the subject, and should undertake to describe it
to you. No language that I could use would give you such
an idea of the painting, as to enable you to form a picture
of it in your minds. Where, on any subject, we are
obliged, from the nature of the case, to use figurative language, analogies, and resemblances, the knowledge we com-
municate is necessarily defective and inadequate. Who of
you have not heard descriptions of persons and places, till
you thought you had an accurate knowledge of them ; but

when you come to see them you find you had no true idea
of the reality ?

Suppose an individual were to visit this world, from
another planet, where all things are constituted on the
most opposite principles from those which are adopted
here; Suppose him to remain here long enough to learn
our language, and that then he should undertake to give
us a description of the world he had left. We should understand it according to our ideas and experience. Now,
if the analogy between the two worlds is very imperfect,
it is plain that our knowledge of things there, from his description, must be imperfect in proportion. So, when we
find in the Bible descriptions of heaven and hell, or anything in the invisible world, it is plain that from mere
words we can get no true ideas at all adequate to the
reality.

2. The wickedness of our hearts is so great, as to per-
vert our judgment, and shut out from our minds much that
we might understand of the things of religion.

When a man's mind is so perverted on any subject, that
he will not take up the evidence concerning it, he cannot,
of course, come at the knowledge of the truth on that subject. This is our case in regard to religion. Perverseness
of heart so shuts out the light, that the intellect does not,
and from the nature of things *cannot*, get even the ideas it
might otherwise gain, respecting divine things.

3. Prejudice is a great obstacle to the reception of correct knowledge concerning religion.

Take the case of the disciples of Christ. They had
strong Jewish prejudices respecting the plan of salvation—
so strong that all the instructions of Christ himself could
not make them understand the truth. After teaching
them personally, for three years, with all the talent, and
simplicity, and skill he was master of, he could never get
their minds in possession of the first principles of the gos-

pel. Up to his very death, he could not make them see that he should die, and rise from the dead. Therefore he says in his last conversation—"If I go not away, the Comforter will not come unto you ; but if I depart, I will send him unto you." This was the very design of his going away from them, that the Spirit of Truth might come, and put them in possession of the things which he meant by the words he had used in teaching them.

The general truth is this ; that without divine illumination, men can understand from the Bible enough to convict and condemn them, but not enough to sanctify and save them.

Some may ask, What, then, is the use of revelation ?

It is of much use. The Bible is as plain as it can be. Who doubts that our Lord Jesus Christ gave instructions to his disciples, as plainly as he could ? See the pains which he took to illustrate his teaching ; how simple his language ; how he brings it down to the weakest comprehension, as a parent would to a little child. And yet it remains true, that without divine illumination, the unaided reason of man never did, and never will attain any available knowledge of the gospel. The difficulty lies in the subject. The Bible contains the gospel, as plain as it can be made. That is, it contains the signs of the ideas, as far as language can represent the things of religion. No language but figurative language can be used for this purpose. And this will for ever be inadequate to put our minds in real possession of the thing themselves. The difficulty is in our ignorance and sin, and in the nature of the subject. This is the reason why we need divine illumination, to get any available knowledge of the gospel.

III. The Spirit of God alone, can give us this illumination.

The Bible says, "No man can say that Jesus Christ is Lord, but by the Holy Ghost." Now the abstract proposition of the Deity of Christ, can be proved, as a matter of science, so as to gain the assent of any unbiassed mind to the truth, that Jesus is Lord. But nothing but the Holy Ghost can so put the mind in possession of the idea of Christ, as God, as to fix the soul in the belief of the fact, and make it available to sanctify the heart.

Again, it is said that "No man can come to me, except the Father which hath sent me draw him ; and I will raise him up at the last day. It is written in the prophets, and they shall be all taught of God. Every man, therefore, that hath heard, and hath learned of the Father, cometh unto me." Here it is evident that the drawing spoken of, is the teaching of the Holy Spirit. They must be taught of God, and learn of the Father, before they can ever have such a knowledge of the things of religion as actually to come to Christ.

Christ says, "It is expedient for you that I go away for if I go not away, the Comforter will not come unto you." The word Παρακλητος, *Paracletos*, here translated Comforter, properly means a Helper, or Teacher. "When he is come, he will reprove the world of sin, and of righteousness, and of judgment : Of sin, because they believe not on me ; of righteousness, because I go to my Father, and ye see me no more ; of judgment, because the prince of this world is judged. I have yet many things to say unto you, but ye cannot bear them now. Howbeit, when he, the Spirit of Truth, is come, he will guide you into all truth ; for he shall not speak of himself ; but whatsoever he shall hear, that shall he speak ; and he will show you things to come."

So in the fourteenth chapter the Saviour says, "I wil pray the Father and he shall give you another Comforter, that he may abide with you forever ; even the Spirit of Truth, whom the world cannot receive, because it seeth him not, neither knoweth him ; but ye know him, for he dwelleth with you, and shall be in you." And again, in the 26th verse, "But the Comforter, which is the Holy Ghost, whom the Father will send in my name, he shall teach you all things, and bring all things to your remembrance, whatsoever I have said unto you." Here you see the office of the Spirit of God is, to instruct mankind in regard to the things of religion.

Now, it is manifest that none but the Spirit of God can supply this defect, from a single consideration—That all teaching by words, whether by Jesus Christ, or by apostles, or by any inspired or uninspired teacher coming merely through the senses, can never put the mind in possession of the idea of spiritual things. The kind of teaching that we need is this; we want some one to teach us the things of religion, who is not obliged to depend on words, or to reach our minds through the medium of the senses. We want some way in which the ideas themselves can be brought to our minds, and not merely the signs of the ideas. We want a teacher who can directly approach the mind itself, and not through the senses; and who can exhibit the ideas of religion, without being obliged to use words. This the Spirit of God can do.

The manner in which the Spirit of God does this, is what we can never know in this world. But the fact is undeniable, that he can reach the mind without the use of words, and can put our minds in possession of the ideas themselves, of which the types, or figures, or words, of the human teacher, are only the signs or imperfect representatives. The human teacher can only use words to our senses, and finds it impossible to possess us of the ideas of that which we have never experienced. But the Spirit of God, having direct access to the mind, can, through the outward sign, possess us of the actual idea of things. What Christian does not know this, as a matter of fact? What Christain does not know, from his own experience, that the Spirit of God does lead him instantly to see that in a passage of scripture, which all his study and effort of mind to know the meaning of could never have given him in the world ?

Take the case again, of a painting on the wall there, and suppose that all the congregation were blind, and I was trying to describe to them this painting. Now, suppose, while I was laboring to make them understand the various distinctions and combination of colors, and they are bending their minds to understand it, all at once their eyes are opened ! You can then see for yourselves the very things which I was vainly trying to bring to your minds by words. Now, the office of the Spirit of God, and what he alone can do, is to open the spiritual eye, and bring the things which we try to describe by analogy and signs, in all their living reality before the mind, so as to put the mind in complete possession of the thing as it is.

It is evident, too, that no one but the Spirit of God so knows the things of God as to be able to give us the idea of those things correctly. " What man knoweth the things of a man, save the spirit of man that is in him ? " What can a beast know of the things of a man, of a man's character, designs, etc. ? I can speak to your consciousness— being a man, and knowing the things of a man. But I cannot speak these things to the consciousness of a beast, neither can a beast speak of these things, because he has not the spirit of a man in him, and cannot know them. In like manner the Bible says, " The things of God knoweth no man, but the Spirit of God." The Spirit of God, knowing from consciousness the things of God, possesses a different kind of knowledge of these things from what other beings can possess ; and therefore, can give us the kind of instruction we need, and such as no other being can give.

IV. The needed influences of the Spirit of God may be possessed by all men, freely, and under the gospel.

A few passages from the Bible will show this :

Jesus Christ says God is more willing to give his Holy Spirit to them that ask him, than parents are to give their children bread. "Ask, and it shall be given you ; seek, and ye shall find ; knock, and it shall be opened unto you." "And all things whatsoever ye shall ask in prayer, believing, ye shall receive." "Therefore I say unto you, What things soever ye desire when ye pray, believe that ye receive them, and ye shall have them." James says, "If any of you lack wisdom, let him ask of God, that giveth to all men liberally, and upbraideth not ; *and it shall be given him.*" If it be true, that God has made these unlimited promises, that *all men,* who will ask of him, may have divine illumination as much as they will ask for, then it is true that all men may have as much of divine illumination as they need.

V. I will show the reasons why any do not have as much divine illumination as they need.

1. They do not ask for it in such a manner or degree as they need it.

2. They ask amiss, or from selfish motives,

The apostle James says, "Ye ask and receive not, because ye ask amiss, that ye may consume it on your lusts." When an individual has a selfish motive for asking, or some other reason than a desire to glorify God, he need not expect to receive divine illumination. If his object in asking for the Holy Ghost, is that he may always be happy in religion, or that he may be very wise in the scriptures, or be looked upon as an eminent Christian, or have his experience spoken of as remarkable, or any other selfish view, that is a good reason why he should not receive even what he asks.

3. They do not use the proper means to attain what they ask.

Suppose a person neglects his Bible, and yet asks God

to give him a knowledge of the things of religion : that is tempting God. The manner in which God gives knowledge is through the Bible, and the other appointed means of instruction. If a person will not use these means, when they are in his power, however much he may pray, he need not expect divine instruction. " Faith cometh by hearing, and hearing by the word of God."

There is an important difference to be observed, between the cases of those who possess these means, and those who do not. I suppose that a person may learn the gospel, and receive all the illumination he needs, under any circumstances of privation of means. As if he was on a desolate island, he might receive direct illumination from the Spirit of God. And so he might, in any other circumstances, where he absolutely could not have access to any means of instruction. Some very remarkable cases of this kind have occurred within a few years. I have known one case, which I looked upon at the time as miraculous, and for that reason have seldom mentioned it, feeling that even the church were not prepared to receive it. When I was an evangelist, I labored once in a revival, in a neighborhood where there were many Germans. They had received but little instruction, and many of them could not read. But when the gospel was preached among them, the Spirit of God was poured out, and a most powerful revival followed. In the midst of the harvest, if a meeting, was appointed at any place, the whole neighborhood would come together, and fill the house, and hang upon the preacher's lips, while he tried to possess their minds with the truth of the gospel. One poor German woman naturally intelligent, but who could not read, in relating her experience in one of these meetings, told this fact which was certified to by her neighbors. With many tears and a heart full of joy, she said, " When I loved God, I longed to read the Bible, and I prayed to Jesus Christ, I said and felt, O Jesus! thou canst teach me to read thy Holy Bible, and the Lord taught me to read. There was a Bible in the house, and when I had prayed, I thought I could read the Bible, and I got the book, and opened it, and the words were just what I had heard people read. I said, 'O Lord Jesus Christ, thou canst teach me to read,' and I believed he could, and I thought I did read, but I went and asked the school-madam if I read, and she said I read it right, and the Lord has taught me to read my Bible, blessed be his name for it." I do not know but the school-madam to whom she referred was in the house and heard her relation. At all events she was a woman of good character among her neighbors, and some of the most respectable of them afterwards told me, they did not doubt the truth of what she said. I have no doubt it was true.

At the time, I thought it was a miracle; but since the facts which have been developed within a few years, respecting the indestructibleness of the memory, I have thought this case might be explained in that way; and that she had probably been told the names of letters and their powers, when young, and now the Spirit of God, in answer to her prayer, had quickened her mind, and brought it all to her remembrance, so that she could read the Bible.

Some of you will recollect the facts which were stated here, one evening, by President Mahan, which show that every impression which is made on the mind of man, remains there for ever indelible. One case that he mentioned was that of an old lady, who, when she was young, had read some lines of poetry, relating a little story; and afterwards, when old, she wished to tell the story to some children, to whom she thought it would be useful, and to her surprise the whole of the lines came up fresh in her memory, and she repeated them word for word, although she had never committed them to memory at all, but only read them when she was young. Another was the case of an ignorant servant girl. She had once lived with a learned minister, who was accustomed to read aloud the Hebrew Bible, in his study, which was in hearing of the place where this girl did her work. Of course she understood nothing of the words, but only heard the sounds. Long afterwards when she was on her death-bed, she astonished the by-standers by reciting whole chapters of Hebrew and Chaldaic. The neighbors at first thought it was a miracle, but at length learned the explanation. It is plain from this, that even unintelligible sound may be so impressed on the memory, as afterwards to recur with entire distinctness. I suppose that was the case with this poor German woman, and that the Spirit of God, in answer to her fervant prayer, so refreshed her memory as to recall the sounds and forms of letters, she had been told when a child, and thus enable ner at once to read the Bible.

I say, therefore, that while those who do not possess any outward means of instruction may obtain directly from the Spirit of God whatever degree or kind of illumination they need in the things of religion ; those who possess or can obtain the outward means, and do not use them, tempt God, when they pray for divine illumination and neglect the use of means for obtaining knowledge. To those who have the opportunity, "faith cometh by hearing, and hearing by the word of God." If any man keeps away from the means within his reach, he can expect illumination in no other way. Whereas, if he is shut out from the use of means, as God is true to his promises, we must believe that he can be illuminated without means, to any extent he needs.

4. Another reason why many do not receive that illumination from the Spirit of God which they need is, because they grieve the Spirit in many ways.

They live in such a manner as to grieve, or offend, the Holy Spirit, so that he cannot consistently grant them his illuminating grace.

5. Another reason is, that they *depend* on the instructions and means, as available without divine influence.

How many rely on the instructions they receive from ministers, or commentaries, or books, or their own powers of inquiry, not feeling that all these things, without the Spirit of God, will only kill, but can never make alive—can only damn, but never save. It seems as though the whole church was in error on this point ; depending on means for divine knowledge, without feeling that no means are available, without the Spirit of God. Oh ! if the church felt this—if they really felt that all the means in creation are unavailing without the teaching of the Holy Ghost, how they would pray, and cleanse their hands, and humble their hearts, until the Comforter would descend to teach them all things that they need to know of religion.

6. Self-confidence is another reason why so little is experienced of divine illumination.

So long as professing Christians place confidence in learning, or criticism, or their natural ingenuity, to learn the things of religion, rely on it, they are not likely to enjoy much of the illumination of the Spirit of God.

VI. I am to show that men are responsible for what they might have of divine illumination.

This is a universal truth, and is acknowledged by all mankind, that a man is just as responsible for what light he might have, as for that he actually has. The common law, which is the voice of common reason, adopts it as a maxim that no man who breaks the law is to be excused for ignorance of the law, because all are held bound to know what the law is. So it is with your children, in a case where they might know your will—you consider them so much the more blameworthy, if they offend. So it is in religion : where men have both the outward means of instruction, and the inward teachings of the Holy Spirit, absolutely within their reach, if they sin ignorantly, they

are not only without excuse on that score, but their **ignor-**
ance is itself a crime, and is an aggravation of their guilt.
And all men are plainly without excuse for not possessing
all the knowledge which would be available for their perfect and immediate sanctification.

CONCLUSION

I. You see what is the effect of all other instructions
on a congregation where no divine influence is enjoyed.

It may convince the church of duty, but will never
produce sanctification. It may harden the heart, but will
never change it. Without divine influence, it is but a
savor of death unto death.

II. You see that it is important to use all the appropriate means of religious instruction in our power, as the
medium through which the Spirit of God conveys divine
illumination to the mind.

There is no reason why we should not use the means in
our power, and apply our natural faculties to acquire
knowledge of religion, as faithfully as if we could understand the whole subject without divine influence. And if
we do not use means, when within our power, we have no
reason to expect divine aid. When we help ourselves,
God helps us. When we use our natural faculties to understand these things, we may expect God will enlighten
us. To turn our eyes away from the light, and then pray
that we may be made to see, is to tempt God.

III. They are blind leaders of the blind, who attempt
to teach the things of religion without being themselves
taught of God.

No degree of learning, or power of discrimination as to
the didactics of theology, will ever make a man a successful teacher of religion, unless he enjoys the illuminating
powers of the Holy Ghost. He is blind if he supposes he
understands the Bible without this, and if he undertakes

to teach religion, he deceives himself, and all who depend on him, and both will fall into the ditch together.

IV. If an individual teaches the gospel with the Holy Ghost sent down from heaven, he will be understood.

He may understand the gospel himself, and yet not make his hearers understand it, because the Holy Ghost is not sent on them as well as on himself. But if the Spirit of God is on them, precisely in proportion as he understands the real meaning of the gospel, he will make his hearers understand it.

V. In preaching the gospel, ministers should never use texts, the meaning of which they have not been taught by the Spirit of the God.

They should not attempt to explain passages of which they are not confident they have been taught the meaning by the Holy Spirit. It is presumption. And they need not do it, for they may always have the teachings of the Spirit, by asking. God is always more ready to bestow divine illumination than an earthly parent is to give bread to his child ; and if they ask as a child when he is hungry asks its mother for bread, they may always receive all the light they need. This is applicable both to preachers and to teachers in Sabbath schools and Bible classes. If any of them attempt to teach the scriptures without being themselves taught, they are no more fit to teach without divine teaching, than the most ignorant person in the streets is fit to teach astronomy. I fear both minister and teachers generally, have understood very little of their *need* of this divine teaching, and have felt very little of the necessity of praying over their sermons and bible lessons, till they feel confident that the Spirit of God has possessed their minds with the true idea of the word of God. If this was done as it ought to be, their instructions would be far more effectual than we now see them. Do you, who are teachers of Bible and Sabbath-school classes in this church, believe this ? Are you in the habit, conscientiously and uniformly, of seeking the true idea of every lesson on your knees ? Or do you go to some commentary, and then come and peddle out your dry stuff to your classes, that you get out of the commentaries and books, without any of the Holy Ghost in your teaching ? If you do this, let me tell you, that you had better be doing something else. What would you say of a minister, if you knew he never prayed over his texts ? You might as well have Balaam's ass for a minister, and even the dumb beast in such a case might speak with man's voice and rebuke the madness of such a man. He could give just as much available instruction to reach the deep fountains of the heart, as such a preacher. Well, now, this is just as important for a Sunday-school teacher as for a minister. If you do not pray over your lesson, until you feel that God has taught you the idea contained in it, *beware!* How dare you go and teach that for religion, which you do not honestly suppose you have been taught of God ?

VI. It is a vast error in theological students, when they study to get the views of all the great teachers, the tomes of the fathers and doctors, and everybody's opinion as to what the Bible means, but the opinion of the Holy Ghost.

With hearts as cold as marble, instead of going right to the source of light, they go and gather up the husks of learning, and peddle it out among the churches as religious instruction. Horrible ! While they do thus, we never shall have an efficient ministry. It is right they should get all the help they can from learning, to understand the word of God. But they ought never to rest in anything they get from book learning, until they are satisfied that God has put them in possession of the very idea which *he* would have them receive.

I have tried hard to make this impression, and I believe I have succeeded in some degree, on the theological students under my care. And if I had done it more, I have no doubt I might have succeeded better. And I can say, that when I studied theology, I spent many hours on my knees, and perhaps I might say weeks, often with the Bible before me, laboring and praying to come at the very mind of the Spirit. I do not say this boastingly, but as a matter of fact, to show that the sentiment here advanced is no novel opinion with me. And I have always got my texts and sermons on my knees. And yet I am conscious that I have gained very little knowledge in religion, compared with what I might have had, if I had taken right hold of the source of light as I ought to have done.

VII. How little knowledge have the great body of the church respecting the word of God!

Put them, for instance, to read the epistles, and other parts, and probably they will not have knowledge enough to give an opinion as to the real meaning of one-tenth of the Bible. No wonder the church is not sanctified! They need *more truth*. Our Saviour says, "Sanctify them through thy truth." This grand means of sanctification must be more richly enjoyed before the church will know what entire sanctification means. The church do not understand the Bible. And the reason is *they have not gone to the author* to explain it. Although they have this blessed privilege every day, and just as often as they choose, of carrying the book right to the author for his explanation; yet how little, how very little, do the church know of the Bible, which they are conscious they have been taught to know by the Holy Ghost! Read the text again, read other similar passages, and then say if Christians are not exceedingly to blame for not understanding the Bible.

VIII. You see the necessity that we should all give ourselves up to the study of the Bible, under divine teaching.

I have recently recommended several books to you to

read, such as Wesley's Thoughts on Christian Perfection, the Memoirs of Brainerd Taylor, Payson, Mrs. Rogers, and others. I have found that, in a certain state of mind, such books are useful to read. But I never pretend to make but *one book* my study. I read them occasionally, but have little time or inclination to read other books much while I have so much to learn of my Bible. I find it like a deep mine, the more I work it, the richer it grows. We must read that more than any or all other books. We must pause and pray over it, verse after verse, and compare part with part, dwell on it, digest it, and get it into our minds, till we feel that the Spirit of God has filled us with the spirit of holiness.

Will you do it ? Will you lay your hearts open to God, and not give him rest, till he has filled you with divine knowledge ? Will you *search* the scriptures ? I have often been asked by young converts, and young men preparing for the ministry, what they should read. *Read the Bible.* I would give the same answer five hundred times. Over and above all other things, study the Bible. It is a sad fact, that most young men, when they enter the ministry often know less of the Bible than of any other book they study. Alas ! alas ! O, if they had the spirit of James Brainerd Taylor, his love for the scriptures, his prayer for divine teaching, we should no longer hear the groans of the churches over the barrenness of so many young preachers, who come out of our seminaries full of book-learning and almost destitute of the Holy Ghost.

SAINTS AT REST

"For we which have believed do enter into rest," —Hebrews 4:3a.

THE following is the course of thought to which I wish to direct your attention this evening :

I. I shall endeavor to show what is *not* the rest here spoken of.

II. Show what it is.

III. Show when we are to enter into this rest.

IV. Show how to come into possession of this rest.

V. Show that all sin consists in, or is caused by, unbelief.

I. I will endeavor to show what is not the rest spoken of in the text.

1. It is evidently not a state of inactivity in religion, that is spoken of in the text under the name of rest.

The apostle who wrote this was very far from being himself inactive in religion, or from encouraging it in others. Those of whom he spoke, including himself, where he says, *we* who have believed, do enter into rest, would know at once that it was not true, that they had entered into the rest of supineness.

2. Neither are we to understand that the perfect rest of heaven is the rest here spoken of.

He speaks of it as a present state, we *do* enter, which was not consistent with the idea that heaven is the rest here spoken of. The perfect rest of heaven includes an absolute freedom from all the pains, trials, sufferings and temptations of this life. The rest of the believer here, may be of the same nature, substantially, with the rest of heaven. It is that rest begun on earth. But it is not made perfect. It differs in some respects, because it does not imply a deliverance from all trials, pains, sickness and death. The apostles and primitive Christians had not escaped these trials, but still suffered their full share of them.

II. I will show what we are to understand by the rest here spoken of.

1. It is rest from controversy with God.

In this sense of cessation from controversy, the word rest, is often used in the Bible. In the context, it is said the children of Israel rested, when they were freed from their enemies. It is cessation from strife or war. Those who enter into this rest cease from their warfare with God, from their struggle against the truth, their war with their own conscience. The reproaches of conscience, that kept them in agitation, the slavish fears of the wrath of God under which men exert themselves as slaves in building up their own works, all are done away. They rest.

2. It implies cessation from our own works.

(1.) Cessation from works performed *for* ourselves.

Much of the apparent religion there is in the world is made up of works done by people which are their own, in this sense. They are working for their own lives—that is, they have this end in view, and are working for themselves, as absolutely as the man who is laboring for his bread. If the object of what you do in religion be, that you may be saved, it matters not whether it is from temporal or eternal ruin, it is for yourself, and you have not ceased from your own works, but are still multiplying works of your own. Now, the rest spoken of in the text, is entire cessation from all this kind of works. The apostle, in verse 10th, affirms this: "He that is entered into his rest, hath ceased from his own works." And in the text, he says, We that believe do enter, or have entered, into rest. It is plain that this rest is ceasing from our own works. Not ceasing from all kind of works, for that is true neither of the saints on earth nor of saints in heaven. We have no reason to believe that any saint or angel, or that God himself, or any holy being is ever inactive. But we cease to perform works with any such design as merely to save our own souls. It is ceasing to work for ourselves, that we may work for God. We are performing our own works, just as long as the supreme object of our works is to be saved. But if the question of our own salvation is thrown entirely on Jesus Christ, and our works are performed out of love to God, they are not our own works.

(2.) In entering into this rest, we cease from all works performed from ourselves, as well as works performed for ourselves.

Works are from ourselves, when they result from the simple, natural principles of human nature, such as conscience, hope, fear, etc., without the influences of the Holy Ghost. Such works are universally and wholly sinful. They are the efforts of selfishness, under the direction of mere natural principles. His conscience convicts him, hope and fear come in aid, and under this influence, the carnal, selfish mind acts. Such acts cannot but be wholly sinful. It is nothing but selfishness. Multiply the forms of selfishness by selfishness for ever, and it will never come to love. Where there is nothing but natural conscience pointing out the guilt and danger, and the constitutional susceptibilities of hope and fear leading to do something, it comes to nothing but the natural workings of an unsanctified mind. Such works are always the works of the flesh, and not the works of the Spirit. To enter into rest is to cease from all these, and no more to perform works from ourselves than for our ourselves. Who does not know what a painful time those have, who set about religion from themselves ; painfully grinding out about so much religion a month, constrained by hope and fear, and lashed up to the work by conscience, but without the least impulse from that divine principle of the love of God shed abroad in the heart by the Holy Ghost ? All such works are just as much from themselves, as any work of any devil is. No matter what kind of works are performed, if the love of God is not the mainspring and life and heart of them, they are our own works, and there is no such thing as rest in them. We must cease from them, because they set aside the gospel. The individual, who is actuated by these prin ciples, sets aside the gospel, in whole or in part. If he i actuated only by these considerations, he sets aside the gospel entirely, and just so far as he is influenced by them, he refuses to receive Christ as his Saviour in that relation. Christ is offered as a complete Saviour, as our Wisdom, Righteousness, Sanctification, and Redemption. And just so far as any one is making efforts to dispense with a Saviour in any of these particulars, he is setting aside the gospel for so much.

(3.) To enter into rest implies that we cease from doing any thing for ourselves.

We are not so much as to eat or drink for ourselves! " Whether, therefore, ye eat or drink, or whatsoever ye do, do all to the glory of God." The man who has entered into this rest, has ceased from doing it. God requires it, and he that has entered into rest has ceased to have any interest of his own. He has wholly merged his own interest in that of Christ. He has given himself so perfectly to Christ, that he has no work of his own to do. There is no reason why he should go about any work of his own. He knows he might as well sit still till he is in hell, as attempt any thing of his own, as to any possibility of saving himself by any exertions of his own. When a man fully understands this, he ceases from making any efforts in this way. See the convicted sinner, how he will strain himself, and put forth all his efforts to help himself, until he learns that he is nothing ; and then he ceases from all this, and throws himself helpless and lost, into the hands of Christ. Until he feels that he is in himself without strength, or help, or hope, for salvation or any thing that tends to it, he will never think of the simplicity of the gospel. No man applies to Christ for righteousness and strength, until he has used up his own, and feels that he is helpless and undone. Then he can understand the simplicity of the gospel plan, which consists in *receiving* salvation, by faith, as a free gift. When he has done all that he could, in his own way, and finds that he has grown no better, that he is no nearer salvation, but rather grown worse, that sin is multiplied upon sin, and darkness heaped upon darkness, until he is crushed down with utter helplessness, then he ceases, and gives all up into the hand of Christ. See that sinner, trying to get into an agony of conviction, or trying to understand religion, and finding all dark as Egypt, and cannot see what it is that he must do. O, says he, what must I do ? I am willing to do any thing. I can't tell why I don't submit, I know not how to do any thing more ; what am I to do, or how shall I find out what is the difficulty ? When he is fully convinced, then he turns his eyes to the Saviour, and there he finds all he needs. Wisdom, Righteousness, Sanctification and Redemption. Christ the Life of the world, the Light of the world, the Bread of life, and he needs nothing of all these but what is in Christ, that all he wants, and all he can ask, is in Christ, and to be received by faith ; then he ceases from his own works, and throws himself at once and entirely upon Christ for salvation.

(4.) To cease from our own works is to cease attempting to do any thing in our own strength.

Every one who has entered into rest knows, that whatever he does in his own strength, will be an abomination to God. Unless Christ lives in him, unless God worketh in him, to will and to do, of his good pleasure, nothing is ever done acceptably to God. To set himself to do any thing in his own strength, independent of the spirit of God, is forever an utter abomination to God. He who has not learned this, has not ceased from his own works, and has not accepted the Saviour. The apostle says, we are not able of ourselves to think anything, as of ourselves. The depth of degradation to which sin has reduced us, is not understood until this is known and felt.

3. To enter into rest also includes the idea of throwing our burdens upon the Lord Jesus Christ.

He invites us to throw all our burdens and cares on him. "Come unto me all ye that labor and are heavy laden, and I will give you rest." "Casting all your cares upon him, for he careth for you." These words mean just as they say. Whether your burden is temporal or spiritual, whether your care is for the soul or body, throw it all upon the Lord. See that little child, going along with his father ; the father is carrying something that is heavy, and the child takes hold with its little hand to help, but what can he do towards carrying such a load ? Many Christians make themselves a great deal of trouble, by trying to help the Lord Jesus Christ in his work. They weary and worry themselves with one thing and another, as if everything hung on their shoulders. Now, the Lord Jesus Christ is as much pledged to the believer for *all* that concerns him, as he is for his justification ; and just as absolutely bound for his temporal as for his eternal interests. There is nothing that concerns the Christian, which he is not to cast on the Lord Jesus Christ. I do not mean to be understood, that the Christian has no agency in the matter. Here is a man who has cast his family upon Jesus Christ ; but he has not done it in any such manner, that he is not to do anything for his family. But he has so cast himself upon God, for direction, for light, for strength, for success, that he has yielded himself up absolutely to God, to guide and to sustain him ; and Christ is pledged to see to it that every thing is done right.

4. To enter into rest is to make the Lord Jesus Christ our wisdom, our righteousness, our sanctification, and our redemption, and to receive him in all his offices, as a full and perfect substitute for all our deficiencies.

We lack all these things, absolutely, and are to receive Him as a full and perfect substitute, to fill the vacancy, and supply all our needs. It is to cease expecting, or hoping, or attempting anything of ourselves, to fill the vacancy ; and receiving Christ as all.

5. Entering into this rest implies the yielding up of our powers so perfectly to his control, that henceforth all our works shall be his works.

I hope you will not understand anything from this language, more mystical than the Bible. It is a maxim of the common law, that what a man does by another, he does by himself. Suppose I hire a man to commit murder ; the deed is as absolutely my own as if I had done it with my own hand. The crime is not in the hand which struck the blow, any more than it is in the sword that stabs the victim. The crime is in my mind. If I use another's hand, if my mind, as the moving cause, influenced him, it is my act still. Suppose that I had taken his hand by force, and used it to shoot my neighbor, would not that be my act ? Certainly ; but it was in my mind, and it is just as much my act, if I influence his mind to do it. Now apply this principle to the doctrine, that the individual who has entered into rest has so yielded himself up to Christ's control, that all his works are the works of Christ. The apostle Paul says, " I labored more abundantly than they all ; yet not I, but the grace of God in me." And he frequently insists upon it, that it was not himself' that did the works, but Christ in him. Do not misunderstand it now. It is not said, and it is not so to be understood, that the believer acts upon compulsion, or that Christ acts in him without his own will, but that Christ by his Spirit dwelling in him, influences and leads his mind that he acts voluntarily in such a way as to please God. When one ceases from his own works, he so perfectly gives up his own will, and places himself so completely under guidance of the Holy Spirit, that whatever he does, is done by the impulse of the Spirit of Christ. The apostle describes it exactly when he says, "Work out your own salvation, with fear and trembling, for it is God that worketh in you, to will and to do of his good pleasure." God influences the will, not by force, but by love, to do just what will please him. If it were done by force, we should be no longer free agents. But it is love that so sweetly influences the will, and brings it entirely under the control of the Lord Jesus Christ.

It is not that our agency is suspended, but is employed by the Lord Jesus Christ. Our hands, our feet, our powers of body and mind, are all employed to work for him. He does not suspend the laws of our constitution, but so directs our agency, that the love of Christ so constrains us, that we will and do of his good pleasure.

Thus, you see that all works that are really good in man, are in an important sense, Christ's works. This is affirmed in the Bible, over and over again, that our good works are not from ourselves, nor in any way by our own agency without God ; but God directs our agency, and influences our wills to do his will, and we do it. They are, in one sense our works, because we do them by our voluntary agency. Yet, in another sense, they are his works, because he is the moving cause of all.

6. Entering into this rest implies, that insomuch as we yield our agency to Christ, insomuch we cease from sin.

If we are directed by the Lord Jesus Christ, he will not direct us to sin. Just as far as we give ourselves up to God we cease from sin. If we are controlled by him, so that he works in us, it is to will and to do of his good pleasure. And just so far as we do this, so far we cease from sin. I need not prove this.

III. I am to inquire when they that believe do enter into rest.

It is in this life.

1. This appears from the text and context. The apostle in connection with the text, was reasoning with the Jews. He warns them to beware, lest they fail of entering into the true rest, which was typified by their fathers entering into the land of Canaan. The Jews supposed that was the true rest. But the apostle argues with them, to show that there was a higher rest of which the rest of temporal Canaan was only a type, and into which the Jews might have entered but for their unbelief. If Joshua had given them the real rest, he would not have spoken of another day. Yet another day is spoken of. Even so late as David's day, it is spoken of in the Psalms as yet to come: "To-day, after so long a time; as it is said To-day if ye will hear his voice, harden not your hearts. For if Jesus (that is Joshua) had given them rest, then would he not afterwards have spoken of another day. There remaineth therefore a rest to the people of God." He therefore argues, that the rest in Canaan was not the real rest which was promised, but was typical of the true rest. What then was the true rest? It was the rest of repose of faith in Christ, or the gospel state, a cessation from our own works. And believers enter into that state by faith.

I know it is generally supposed that the rest here spoken of is the heavenly rest, beyond this life. But it is manifestly a rest that commences here. "We which believe *do* enter into rest." It begins here, but extends into eternity. It is the same in kind, but made there more perfect in degree, embracing freedom from the sorrows and trials to which all believers are subject in this life. But it is the same in kind, the rest of faith, the Sabbath keeping of the soul when it ceases from its own works, and casts itself wholly upon the Saviour.

2. It is manifest that this rest must commence in this world, if faith puts us in possession of it. This is the very point that the apostle was arguing, that faith is essential to taking possession of it. They " could not enter in because of unbelief." " Beware, least ye fail of entering in after the same example of unbelief." He warns them not to indulge in unbelief, because by faith they may take immediate possession of the rest. If this rest by faith ever commences at all, it must be in this world.

3. The nature of the case proves this. Nothing short of this taking possession of rest is fully embracing Jesus Christ. It is a spiritual rest from the conflict with God, from the stings of conscience, and from efforts to help ourselves by any workings of our own mind. Nothing short of this is getting clear away from the law, or entering fully into the gospel.

IV. I am show *how* we are to enter into this rest.

From what has already been said, you will understand that we take possession of it by faith.

The text, with the context, show this. You will recollect also what the Lord Jesus Christ says, Matthew xi. 28. 29. " Come unto me all ye that labor and are heavy laden, and I will give you rest. Take my yoke upon you, and learn of me : for I am meek and lowly in heart ; and ye shall find rest unto your souls." Here this same rest is spoken of, and we are told that if we will only come to Christ we may find it. If we will take his easy yoke, which is love, and trust him to bear all burdens, we shall find rest. The Psalmist speaks of the same rest—" Return unto thy rest, O my soul." What Christain does not know what it is to have the soul rest in Christ, to hang upon his arm, and find rest from all the cares and perplexities and sorrows of life ?

Again : It is evident that faith in Christ, from its own nature, brings the soul into the very state of rest I have described. How instantly faith breaks up slavish fear, and brings the soul into the liberty of the gospel ! How it sets us free from selfishness, and all those influences we formerly acted under ! By faith we confide all to Christ, to lead us, and sanctify us, and justify us. And we may be just as certain to be led and to be sanctified, as we are to be justified, if we only exercise faith and leave ourselves in the hands of Christ for all. As a simple matter of fact, such faith brings the soul into a state of rest. The soul sees that there is no need of its own selfish efforts, and no hope from them if they were needed. In itself, it is so far gone in sin that it is as hopeless as if it had been in hell a thousand years. Take the best Christian on earth, and let the Lord Jesus Christ leave his soul, and where is he ? Will he pray or do anything good, or acceptable to God, without Christ ? Never. The greatest saint on earth will go right off into sin in a moment, if abandoned by Jesus Christ. But faith throws all upon Christ, and that is rest.

Again : Faith makes us cease from all works for ourselves. By faith we see that we have no more need of doing works for ourselves, than the child needs to work for his daily bread whose father is worth millions. He may work, from love to his father, or from love to the employment, but not from any necessity to labor for his daily bread. The soul that truly understands the gospel, sees perfectly well that there is no need of mingling his own righteousness with the righteousness of Christ, or his own wisdom with the wisdom of Christ, or his own sufferings with the sufferings of Christ. If there was any need of this, there would be just so much temptation to selfishness, and to working from legal motives. But there is none.

Again : By faith the soul ceases from all works performed from itself. Faith brings a new principle into action, entirely above all considerations addressed to the natural principles of hope and fear and conscience. Faith brings the mind under the influence of love. It takes the soul out from the influences of conscience, lashing it up to duty, and brings it under the influence of the same holy, heavenly principles, that influenced Christ himself.

Again : Faith brings the mind into rest, inasmuch as it brings it to cease from all efforts merely for its own salvation, and puts the whole being into the hands of Christ.

Faith is confidence. It is yielding up all our powers and interests to Christ, in confidence, to be led, and sanctified, and saved by him.

It annihilates selfishness, and thus leaves no motives for our own works.

In short : Faith is an absolute resting of the soul in Christ, for all that it needs, or can need. It is trusting him for every thing. For instance—Here is a little child, wholly dependent on its father, for house and home, food and raiment, and every thing under the sun. Yet that little child feels no uneasiness, because it confides in its father. It rests in him, and gives itself no uneasiness, but that he will provide all that it needs. It is just as cheerful and happy, all the day long, as if it had all things in itself, because it has such confidence. Now the soul of the believer rests in Christ, just as the infant does on the arms of it mother. The penitent sinner, like a condemned wretch, hangs all on Christ, without the least help or hope, only as they come from Christ alone, and as Christ does all that is needed.

If faith does consist in thus trusting absolutely in Christ, then it is manifest that this rest is taken possession of when we believe ; and that it must be in this life, if faith is to be exercised in this life.

V. I am to show that unbelief is the cause of all the sin there is in the world.

I do not mean to imply by this, that unbelief is not itself a sin; but to say, that it is the fountain out of which issues all other sin. Unbelief is distrust of God, or want of confidence. It is manifest that it was this want of confidence which constituted Adam's real crime. It was not the mere eating of the fruit, but the distrust which led to the outward act, that constituted the real crime for which he was cast out of Paradise. That unbelief is the cause of all sin is manifest from the following considerations:

The moment an individual wants faith, and is left to the simple impulse of natural principles and appetites, he is left just like a beast, and the things that address his mind through the senses alone operate on him. The motives that influence the mind when it acts right, are discerned by faith. Where there is no faith, there are no motives before the mind but such as are confined to this world. The soul is then left to its mere constitutional propensities, and gives up itself to the minding of carnal things. This is the natural and inevitable result of unbelief. The eye is shut to eternal things, and there is nothing before the mind calculated to beget any other action but that which is selfish. It is therefore left to grovel in the dust, and can never rise above its own interest and appetites. It is a natural impossibility that the effect should not be so; for how can the mind act without motives? But the motives of eternity are seen only by faith. The mere mental and bodily appetites that terminate on this world, can never raise the mind above the things of this world, and the result is only sin, sin, sin—the minding of the flesh for ever. The very moment Adam distrusted God, he was given up to follow his appetites. And it is so with all other minds.

Suppose a child loses all confidence in its father. He

can henceforth render no hearty obedience. It is a natural impossibility. If he pretends to obey, it is only from self-ishness, and not from the heart ; for the mainspring and essence of all real hearty obedience is gone. It would be so in heaven, it is so in hell. Without faith it is impossi-ble to please God. It is a natural impossibility to obey God in such a manner as to be accepted of him, without faith. Thus unbelief is shown to be the fountain of all the sin in earth and hell, and the soul that is destitute of faith, is just left to work out its damnation.

CONCLUSION

I. The rest which those who believe do enter into here on earth, is of the same nature with the heavenly rest.

The heavenly rest will be more complete ; for it will be a rest from all the sorrows and trials to which even a perfect human soul is liable here. Even Christ himself experienced these trials and sorrows and temptations. But the soul that believes, rests as absolutely in him here, as in heaven.

II. We see why faith is said to be the substance of things hoped for.

Faith is the very thing that makes heaven ; and there-fore it is the substance of heaven, and will be to all eternity.

III. We see what it is to be led by the Spirit of God.

It is to yield up all our powers and faculties to his con-trol, so as to be regulated by the Spirit in all that we do.

IV. We see that perfect faith would produce perfect love, or perfect sanctification.

A perfect yielding up of ourselves, and continuing to trust all that we have and are to Christ, would make us perfectly holy.

V. We see that just as far as any individual is not sanctified, it is because his faith is weak.

When the Lord Jesus Christ was on earth, if his disciples fell into sin, he always reproached them with a want of faith : "O ye of little faith." A man that believes in Christ has no more right to expect to sin, than he has a right to expect to be damned. You may startle at this, but it is true.

You are to receive Christ as your sanctification, just as absolutely as for your justification. Now you are bound to expect to be damned, unless you receive Christ as your justification. But if you receive him as such, you have then no reason and no right to expect to be damned. Now he is just as absolutely your sanctification, as your justification, and if you depend upon him for sanctification, he will no more let you sin, than he will let you go to hell. And it is as unreasonable, and unscriptural and wicked, to expect one as the other. And nothing but unbelief, in any instance, is the cause of your sin. Some of you have read the Life of Mrs. Hester Ann Rogers, and recollect how habitual it was with her, when any temptation assailed her, instantly to throw herself upon Christ ; and she testifies, that in every instance he sustained her.

Take the case of Peter. When the disciples saw Christ walking upon the water, after their affright was over, Peter requested to be permitted to come to him on the water, and Christ told him to come ; which was a promise on the part of Christ that if he attempted it, he should be sustained. But for this promise, his attempt would have been tempting God. But with this promise, he had no reason and no right to doubt. He made the attempt, and while he believed, the energy of Christ bore him up, as if he had been walking upon the ground. But as soon as he began to doubt, he began to sink. Just so it is with the soul ; as soon as it begins to doubt the willingness and the power of Christ to sustain it in a state of perfect love, it begins to sink. Take Christ at his word, make him responsible, and rely on him, and heaven and earth will sooner fail than he will allow such a soul to fall into sin. Say, with Mrs. Rogers, when Satan comes with a temptation, "Lord Jesus, here is a temptation to sin, see thou to that."

VI. You see why the self-denying labors of saints are consistent with being in a state of rest,

These self-denying labors are all constrained by love, and have nothing in them that is compulsory or hard. Inward love draws them to duty. So far is it from being true, that the self-denying labors of Christians are hard work, that it would be vastly more painful to them *not* to do it. Their love for souls is such, that if they were forbidden to do any thing for them, they would be in agony. In fact, a state of inaction would be inconsistent with this rest. How could it be rest, for one whose heart was burning and bursting with love to God and to souls to sit still and do nothing for them. But it is perfect rest for the soul to go out in prayer and effort for their salvation. Such a soul cannot rest, while God is dishonored and souls destroyed, and nothing done for their rescue. But when all his powers are used for the Lord Jesus Christ, this is true rest. Such is the rest enjoyed by angels, who cease not day nor night, and who are all ministering spirits, to minister to the heirs of salvation.

The apostle says, "Take heed, therefore, lest a promise being left of entering into rest, any of you should come short of it." And "Let us labor therefore, to enter into rest." Do any of you know what it is to come to Christ, and rest in him ? Have you found rest, from all your own efforts to save yourselves, from the thunders of Sinai, and the stings of conscience ? Can you rest sweetly in Jesus, and find in him every thing essential to sanctification and eternal salvation ? Have you found actual salvation in him ? If you have, then you have entered into rest.

Captive Hearts

Story & Art by
Matsuri Hino

Vol. 2

Captive Hearts
Vol. 2

CONTENTS

Captive Hearts by MATSURI HINO

THE STORY THUS FAR...

PRESENT DAY. KURONEKOMARU'S DESCENDANT, YOSHIMI KUROISHI, WORKS FOR THE KOGAMI FAMILY AS A BUTLER...

happy

What?

THE KOGAMI FAMILY'S GUARDIAN DEITY, THE DRAGON GOD, APPEARED AND CURSED KURONEKOMARU AND HIS DESCENDANTS TO SERVE THE KOGAMI FAMILY FOR A HUNDRED GENERATIONS AS PUNISHMENT...

HOWEVER...

...AN INFAMOUS THIEF CALLED "KURO-NEKOMARU" STOLE "THE SCROLL OF THE RISING DRAGON" FROM THE WEALTHY KOGAMI FAMILY.

A LONG TIME AGO DURING THE MURO-MACHI PERIOD...

Nooo, Master! Mistress! Miss Suzuka!

FOURTEEN YEARS AGO, THE KOGAMI FAMILY WENT MISSING DURING A TRIP TO CHINA, AND KUROISHI RECEIVED WORD THAT THE WHOLE FAMILY WAS DEAD.

Ni hao

I'm so relieved! She's safe!!

SUZUKA, THE 17-YEAR-OLD DAUGHTER AND ONLY SURVIVING MEMBER OF THE KOGAMI FAMILY, CAME BACK HOME TO JAPAN FROM CHINA.

But then...

...WAS LIVING A LEISURELY COLLEGE STUDENT'S LIFE THANKS TO THE KOGAMI FORTUNE AND WAS UNAWARE OF THE "SERVANT CURSE."

(20 years old?)

YOSHI-MI'S SON, 20-YEAR-OLD MEGUMI...

Meanwhile...

WHEN HIS EYES MEET SUZUKA'S, HIS PERSONALITY CHANGES AND HE HAS A SEVERE "MAN-SERVANT FIT."

I'm ready for your orders!

Princess...!

The first time he heard the truth.

BUT IN HIS CASE, HE HAD LIVED WITHOUT THE CURSE FOR SO LONG THAT HE HAD AN INCREDIBLE REACTION TO IT.

Heh heh... Actually, Megumi...

BEFORE LONG, MEGUMI BEGAN EXPERIENCING THE EFFECTS OF THE CURSE AS WELL.

AT FIRST MEGUMI HATED IT, BUT NOW HE LOVES SUZUKA VERY MUCH. AND SUZUKA FEELS THE SAME WAY ABOUT HIM...

...SUZUKA FELT UNEASY BECAUSE SHE THOUGHT I WAS DOING THESE THINGS **ONLY** BECAUSE OF THE CURSE.

WHILE UNDER THE INFLUENCE OF THE CURSE, NO MATTER HOW NICE OR DEVOTED I WAS, OR HOW MANY TIMES I SAID "I LOVE YOU"...

THIS HAPPENED RECENTLY...

A little UNEASY

How does Megumi really feel?

SUZUKA! SUZUKA! SUZUKA!

WHEN WE'RE APART...

...YOU TEND TO DO RECKLESS THINGS.

THAT'S WHY SHE ORDERED ME TO TELL HER MY TRUE FEELINGS.

Tell me your true feelings. It's an order!

PANIC! Arrrrgh!

SHE LOVES ME (WHICH MAKES ME SO HAPPY! ♡) SO THAT MADE HER FEEL EVEN MORE UNEASY.

Note: When a member of the Kuroishi family is under the curse's influence, he/she cannot disobey an order from a Kogami, no matter what!!

SUZUKA REALLY REGRETTED DOING IT...

I'm sorry, Megumi!

I'll tell you my true feel-...now!

Prin-cess

Heh heh heh

About to tell his true feelings regardless of Suzuka's protests

Scary "Following Orders" Mode!

If you tell me your true feelings because I ordered you to, I'll...

On top of the school roof

SUZUKA REALLY RESPECTS MY WISHES.

GASP

Back to normal

SINCE CARRYING OUT THE ORDER WOULD ENDANGER SUZUKA'S LIFE, IT WAS REVOKED.

I LEARNED THAT THE HARD WAY THE OTHER DAY...

7

THERE WAS THE JIE WEN...

AND...

AND ALSO...

And...

YOU TOUCH ME ALL THE TIME, LIKE RIGHT NOW!

You...

SHE'S SO SERIOUS, NAIVE AND STUBBORN, BUT SHE'S A GOOD PERSON.

..."JIE WEN"?

Chinese again...

BLUUSH

Oh.

Also embarrassed.

nod nod

BLUUSH

BLUUSH

THE KISS...?

TWITCH

DURING THE 14 YEARS SHE WAS MISSING, SHE LIVED IN CHINA...

DOING THAT...

Depressed

WAS IT THAT BAD?!

...AND WAS DEEPLY INFLUENCED BY THE CULTURE OF THE PARENTS THAT RAISED HER.

DOING THAT...

PRIN-CESS...

Warning: Megumi is now having a **Manservant Fit.**

Megumi...

Please act normal!!

WELL THEN...

PLEASE...

MARRY M—

IF YOU FALL ON YOUR HEAD, YOU'LL DIE!!

Kyaaa

HANG ON, MEGU-MI!

kyaaa

FWOOP

HE'S BACK TO NORMAL...

Phew.

wobble wobble

YOU... YOU SAVED ME.

I CAN'T... NOT AS LONG AS I HAVE THIS STUPID CURSE... RIGHT?

THAT WAS CLOSE! WHAT WAS I SAYING?

dizzy

MARRIAGE?!

AFTER ALL, I HAVE MY PRIDE AS A MAN.

I WANT TO LIVE WITH SUZUKA WITH MONEY I'VE EARNED MYSELF.

...WHAT?

...WORKING AS A SERVANT HERE...

...IF I SHOULD GET A JOB...

I WON-DER...

whisper

Kuroishi-san the butler

AND THAT...

...IS JUST A SIMPLE INTRODUCTION.

...IS MADE UP OF NUMEROUS COMPANIES THAT HAVE BEEN SUCCESSFUL EVEN DURING RECESSIONS.

THEY'RE LEADERS IN THE BUSINESS WORLD.

THE TAKATSUKASA GROUP...

...AND THERE ARE RUMORS THAT HE'LL ONE DAY SUCCEED HIM.

HIRYU-SAMA HERE IS THE ONLY SON OF THE TAKATSUKASA GROUP'S CHAIRMAN...

IN OTHER WORDS, HE'S A RICH KID.

Wow...

Right?

THAT'S CORRECT.

YOU!!

And more importantly...

SHE WAS RAISED IN CHINA...

SUZUKA ISN'T THE TYPE OF WOMAN YOU RICH KIDS CAN PLAY AROUND WITH.

MARRIAGE ISN'T SOMETHING TO JOKE ABOUT!

HEY, HEY...

nod nod

SNAP

WHOOSH

TWITCH

sticking together

17

It won't end up like that...

Okay...

Don't cry... We're just listening to what he has to say.

I...

...YOU CAN BRING YOUR FAMILY TOO!

HOW ABOUT THAT?

I GOT IT!

WHEN YOU COME TO BE MY BRIDE...

WHAT...?

Huh?

I TURNED 16 THE OTHER DAY.

I'M AFRAID YOU LOOK YOUNGER THAN 18 YEARS OLD, SO...

What's the ... ?!!

HE'S ONE YEAR YOUNGER THAN SUZUKA!

I AM ACTING AS MISS SUZUKA'S GUARDIAN IN PLACE OF HER LATE PARENTS...

...AND I THINK WE SHOULD DISCUSS THIS WITH YOUR PARENTS AT A LATER TIME.

BOW

EX-CUSE ME FOR BEING FRANK, BUT...

BOOM

Ah

20

The 2nd volume of this silly manga is out...

blush

I'm so happy ... Eh heh heh...

This is Matsuri Hino. Thanks for picking this book up!

Thanks to my mom, my friends, my assistants and of course, the readers. This is volume 2!

In this manga, there are two special features.

#1: There are TWO summaries!

#2: There are bonus comic strips!!

...What do you think?

MEGUMI ...?

IN OTHER WORDS...

IN HIS EYES, OUR RELATION-SHIP IS SIMPLY THAT...

...YOU ARE MY MIS-TRESS...

glide

...AND I AM MERELY YOUR SERVANT.

I DON'T MIND THOUGH.

HE JUST SHOWED ME THE REALITY OF THE SITUATION.

Totally normal.

NOT REALLY.

ARE YOU... HAVING A FIT RIGHT NOW?

HM?

MEGUMI...

IT SUDDENLY OCCURRED TO ME...

BUT...

...THAT MAYBE YOU'D BE HAPPIER WITH SOMEONE LIKE TAKATSUKASA.

Don'

DON'T ACCEPT THAT KIND OF REALITY...

...SO EASILY!

TMP

...

TMP TMP TMP TMP

THAT'S HONESTLY WHAT I THOUGHT...

I CAN'T HELP IT...

ARGGH~~!

...MARRIAGE PRO- POSALS!

...HAVE BEEN SENDING YOU SO MANY...

LATELY, GUYS LIKE HIM...

"Because..."

SIGH

IN ANY CASE...

Idiot!

With all her might!

I'M SO HAPPY... I HOPE SHE DOESN'T HOLD BACK AND SAYS WORDS LIKE THAT MORE OFTEN!

EMBAR- RASSED

...I'VE EVER HEARD SUZUKA SAY "IDIOT" AND "HATE."

THAT WAS THE FIRST TIME...

SUZUKA ?!

GASP

SUZUKA-SAN'S KNIGHT RUSHES TO HER SIDE, AS EXPECTED.

OH, NO...

HE'S JUST NOT A VERY CALM PERSON...

Ha ha ha.

DID THAT MAN...

...DO SOMETHING TO YOU?

YOU FELL ON IT, RIGHT?

Well, look.

DENTED

MEGU MU

MM...

You've really done it...!

N... NO...

We got a bill for the cost of repairing that car...

It's a Porsche...

Invoice

¥2,118,000—
($19,240—)

¥2,118,000—

Ka—ching!

A maniac about saving money.

Values money as a commoner does since she was living in China.

I guess I did...

Just a student who mooches off his parents.

YES, MASTER HIRYU.

LET'S GO, SHIBATA!

THAT'S ENOUGH MONEY TO BUY A NEW CAR...

I-IS IT SO EXPENSIVE BECAUSE I FELL ON IT TOO?

WHO ARE YOU?

?

KLUNK

OH, I'M SORRY.

OH...

...SO WE GAVE YOU A DISCOUNT.

smile

Oh, yes.

YOU APOLO-GIZED SO NICELY, SUZUKA...

33

RELATED...

...BY BLOOD...

...TO ME...?

MASTER MINATO...

I HUMBLY APOLOGIZE FOR NOT REALIZING IT SOONER.

NOT AT ALL, KUROISHI-SAN!

I SUPPOSE THAT MAKES US SECOND COUSINS...

I'M ONLY A LOW-RANKING EMPLOYEE OF THE TAKATSU-KASA GROUP.

AND NOW I SERVE MASTER HIRYU...

...AS HIS GUARDIAN.

TELL ME SOME-THING...

HEY.

HE'S... JUST IN A STATE OF SHOCK IS ALL!

limp

NO!

THAT GUY THAT FREAKED OUT OVER THE CAR REPAIRS... IS HE SICKLY OR SOMETHING?

NOT FINE.

Megu-mi

...I SEE.

THAT'S FINE THEN.

BECAUSE I'VE NEVER...

KICK!

YOU'RE THE ONE WHO WOULDN'T LET GO OF MISS SUZUKA'S HAND WHILE YOU WERE ESCAPING REALITY!

THEY...

...WORRIED?

I CAN'T BELIEVE I WAS ACTUALLY WORRIED!!

WHY ARE YOU ALWAYS SO THOUGHTLESS?!

STOMP

THEY'RE GONE NOW...

NO WAY... HE'S NEVER LIKE THAT...

KUROISHI-SAN WAS A NERVOUS WRECK!

What are you babbling on about?!

SO SOFT...

HOW DID I END UP HERE...?

In heaven

HIRYU-KUN LOOKED WORRIED TOO.

OH... I SEE...

MINATO-SAN, YOU'RE MY SECOND COUSIN, SO THAT MEANS YOUR MOTHER IS PAPA'S COUSIN...

MY MOM WAS A SINGLE MOTHER...

...AND SHE WORKED AS MASTER HIRYU'S PERSONAL MAID FOR YEARS...

HOW-EVER...

WHAT A SHAME...

SO HOW IS GREAT AUNT HARUKO?

THE ONLY ONE THERE BY HER SIDE WAS MASTER HIRYU...

FOUR YEARS AGO, SHE COLLAPSED AT WORK WITH A HEART ATTACK.

SHE DIED OF OLD AGE LAST YEAR.

AND HE...

...GAVE HER CPR AND CALLED AN AMBULANCE.

s;p
s;p
...

AND AT HIS REQUEST, SHE WAS TAKEN TO THE BEST HOSPITAL AND RECEIVED EXCELLENT MEDICAL CARE.

IT'S BECAUSE OF HIM THAT MY MOTHER'S LIFE WAS SAVED.

YOU LOOK SO MUCH LIKE MISTRESS HARUKO...

OH... WELL...

I NEVER INTENDED TO TELL ANYONE ABOUT IT...

BUT HOW DID YOU RECOGNIZE ME?

glance

Actually due to him ♭♭

MINATO-SAN...YOUR MOTHER IS REALLY IMPORTANT TO YOU, ISN'T SHE?

UM...

REALLY?

BUT YOU LOOK LIKE YOUR MOM, NOT YOUR GRANDMA...

Hmph,

46

I HAVE AN OEDIPUS COMPLEX.

YES.

DON'T TELL PEOPLE YOU HAVE AN OEDIPUS COMPLEX!

HEY...!

I...

...REALLY WANT SUZUKA.

...AND WE NO LONGER HAVE THE PROTECTION OF THE KOGAMI GUARDIAN DEITY.

WE HAVEN'T BEEN IN CONTACT WITH HER FAMILY FOR AGES...

I DIDN'T KNOW YOU WERE RELATED TO SUZUKA...

HMPH...

I'M SORRY, I GOT CARRIED AWAY.

47

SAY WHAT-EVER YOU WANT.

Hmph

I HAVE NO INTENTION OF LOSING TO YOU.

First son: Hiryu

Passing by after taking a bath

JUST SO YOU KNOW, MY HUSBAND IS MUCH MORE RESPECTED THAN YOU.

I'M GOING TO WIN ON MY OWN, MEIKO.

SHUT UP ALREADY...

Tch.

A BIT OVER-CONFIDENT, AREN'T WE, NANAMI?

MASTER HIRYU... JUST BE PATIENT FOR A BIT LONGER...

ALL THE ELDERS CARE ABOUT IS HIRYU, BUT WHAT ABOUT US?

IT'S NOT FAIR.

49

--To mama in China--

I have some great news.

We found a blood relative of mine.

Minato-san treasures his mother, honors his promises, and is a good person.

But the "Servant's Curse" still exists...

...so I'm worried about Megumi. Do you think there's a way to break the curse?

HUH?

Oh, no! What should I do?

M-Megumi is sick!

HEY, YOU OVER THERE! SERVANT!!

I'M JUST DOING AS DAD SAYS...

I am not!

SET THE TABLE LIKE I TOLD YOU TO! AND DO IT RIGHT!

Yes, sir!

GOOD MORNING, MISS SUZUKA! YOU SEE...

Oh.

KUROISHI-SAN, WHY...?

I PAID THE BILL IN PLACE OF MEGUMI.

Invoice
¥2,118,000—
(Bill for the Porsche's repairs)
from Minato Shibata ♡

W-WHAT? WHAT NOW?

b-bump

IS HE HAVING ANOTHER "MANSERVANT FIT"? NO, SOMETHING'S DIFFERENT...

BUT...

HE'S ALWAYS DAZED THIS EARLY...

THE MEGUMI I KNOW IS NEVER THIS ON TOP OF THINGS IN THE MORNING...

56

TH-
TH-
UMP

SHA

MINATO-
SAN!

PLEASE
STOP!

STOP
THIS...

I WAS
TRYING TO
DAMAGE YOUR
RELATIONSHIP
JUST A LITTLE
SO I COULD
HELP MASTER
HIRYU...

IT JUST
SLIPPED
OUT...

...

I'M
SORRY.

68

69

THE TAKATSU-KASA MANSION

I'M HERE LIKE I PROMISED!

SO TELL ME!

TELL ME HOW TO BREAK THE SERVANT'S CURSE!

NO WAY.

...ENGAGE-MENT?

BUT IF YOU AGREE TO ANNOUNCE YOUR ENGAGEMENT TO MASTER HIRYU, I'LL TELL YOU.

I HAVE NO PROBLEM LYING FOR MASTER HIRYU'S SAKE.

YOU LIAR...!

WHAT!?

...Engage-ment?

71

MEGUMI WOULD PROBABLY SAY THERE'S NO REASON TO GO TO SUCH LENGTHS TO BREAK THE CURSE...

HE'S PROBABLY WORRIED.

...!

GRRR... IDIOT!

flop

Translation:

SLAM

I was tricked.

SHANG DANG LE...

(That's what she said.)

BUT...

I DON'T WANT TO GET ENGAGED TO HIRYU...

...BUT I DON'T WANT MEGUMI TO BE CURSED FOREVER EITHER!

HE'S...

HE'S A KOGAMI TOO, SO I THOUGHT ...!!

!

rattle rattle

NOK NOK NOK

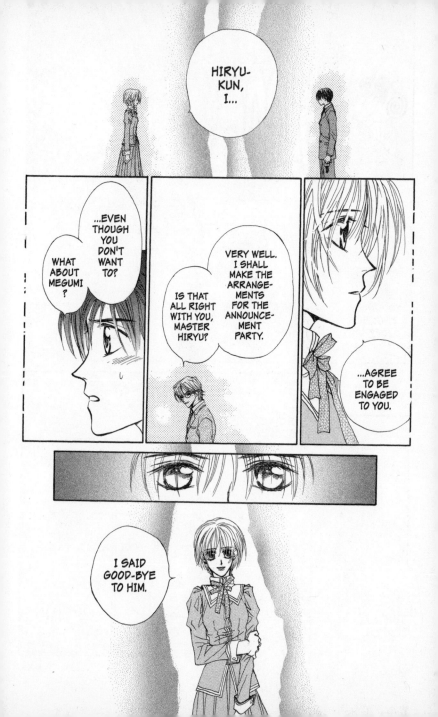

GLOOMY

IT'S BECAUSE YOU TOLD MISS SUZUKA YOU WERE BACKING OFF!!

You've been like this ever since she left!

Aggh?! How depressing!

Muxxu

SUZUKA ABANDONED ME...

SULLEN

BUT AT THE TIME, IT SEEMED LIKE I HAD TO.

I DON'T KNOW WHY I SAID IT THOUGH...

WHO IS THIS FROM...?

Maimam

EXPRESS DELIVERY!

TMP

It might be Suzuka !!

Ah!! Ah!!

OH, MY!

Hmph.

OH, I'LL GO.

AND I'LL SEE FOR MYSELF WHETHER THIS IS WHAT SUZUKA TRULY WANTS OR SOMETHING SHIBATA SET UP.

YOU LOOK BEAUTIFUL...!

...XIE XIE.

79

HMM? WHERE'S MINATO-SAN...?

glance

HE WENT TO PICK GRANDPA UP AT THE AIRPORT.

SO CUTE...

Peek

WHAT DO YOU THINK, HIRYU-KUN?

THE PARTY WILL START SOON.

HIRYU-KUN, AREN'T YOU GOING TO CHANGE?

I LOVE YOU.

YOU HAVEN'T SAID IT.

...TOLD ME YOU LOVE ME.

WHAT?

th-thump

BUT YOU HAVEN'T...

THAT'S...

...WHAT I'VE TOLD YOU OVER AND OVER AGAIN...

HA HA! HA HA HA!

CHATTER

Hyuuuu

KNOWING THAT...

...CAN YOU STILL TRUST ME?

IT'S DONE!

I HAVE TO DO IT NOW!

glance

2!

Ahhh!!

Fshuun !

I'LL CUT THE ELECTRICITY TO MAKE EVERYONE PANIC...

...AND THEN YOU GO GET MISS SUZUKA!!

IT'S FREEZING!

84

3

Reason behind the names.

<#1>
You might already know this though... ♪

In Kuroishi-san's family, both boys and girls were given first names with only one kanji character. Not only that, but it seems they were given names that could be used for either girls or boys. The reason is a mystery!

<#2>
You might already know this too... ♪♪

In the Takatsukasa family, all the children were given a name where one kanji character had the "sanzui" or "water" radical. The reason is a mystery!

Also, I got the idea for Hiryu's sister's name (Meiko) from a coworker when I used to work at a bookstore. Thanks, Meiko-saaan! ♪
↳ What a pretty name... ♡

● ● ●

Why am I so obsessed with meanings behind names? Maybe it's because I had a hard time with my own name (my real name) growing up? I don't know. The reason is a mystery!

... SUZUKA!

I'M SORRY I RAN AWAY FROM HOME!

I MISSED YOU TOO!

I MISSED YOU SO MUCH ...!

Megumi let me go!

HERE.

sha

.....

sigh...

?

IT'S WHAT I PROMISED.

What?!

SHIBATA.

...SO I NO LONGER NEED THIS.

MY PLAN ALREADY FAILED...

WHERE DO YOU THINK YOU'RE GOING?

WHAT does?!

chuckle

I HOPE IT WORKS.

97

AFTER YOU'RE DONE, YOU'LL COME BACK TO ME, RIGHT?

MASTER HIRYU...

BUT I...

BUT...

YOU DID THE THING I HATE THE MOST.

THAT'S RIGHT.

...I STILL TRUST YOU.

YES, SIR...

HE'S REALLY UPSET...

LET'S FACE GRANDFATHER TOGETHER.

SO PLEASE.

98

THE CURSE DIDN'T BREAK WHEN WE KISSED BEFORE!

STOP.

MEGU-MI... MAYBE IT'S... IMPOS-SIBLE?

...

She saw through it.

NO...

...BUT IT'S KIND OF DISAPPOINTING!

...AFTER HE GOES CRAZY FROM A KOGAMI'S ORDER!

IT TELLS HOW YOU TURN A KUROISHI BACK TO NORMAL...

However, this method...

Somehow, the kiss made the order null and void.

After trying 98 different things to wake her up, he finally succeeded with the 99th approach: a kiss.

One day, he ordered his workaholic servant Kaname Kuroishi to go to sleep.

This is a method that my great-grandfather, Gorota Kogami, accidentally discovered.

Ha Ha ha ha ha

Who are you?!

W 9

...is a little weird when used between the same sex.

The author's struggles due to Captive Hearts.

(It's not really a struggle.)

Captive Hearts

For first-time readers of Captive Hearts — Primer Course

IT'S NOT A SCARY STORY.

DON'T WORRY,

At any rate. Timeline of events before the protagonist, Megumi Kuroishi, was taken captive.

As long as he looks after the mansion for them, I can live a life of luxury!

I'm so lucky that the Kogami family went missing and my dad works here!

When Megumi was oblivious to the curse...

Master, Mistress, where are youuu...?

It's sad that her parents died though.

A Kogami is alive? What a terrible development!

I'm so relieved! so relieved! so relieved!

GRIN

I'm your servant, Princess!

And then Suzuka appeared...

Megumi is controlled by the "Servant's Curse."

THEN...

How can we break the curse...?

Muromachi Period	• MEGUMI'S ANCESTOR, THE GREAT THIEF "KURONEKOMARU," STEALS "THE SCROLL OF THE RISING DRAGON" FROM THE KOGAMI MANSION.
	• THE DRAGON GOD APPEARS FROM THE SCROLL AND SAYS, "FOR A HUNDRED GENERATIONS, YOU AND YOUR DESCENDANTS SHALL SERVE THE KOGAMI FAMILY WITH YOUR BODY AND SOUL", AND *CURSES* THEM.
Edo Period	• LOTS OF STUFF HAPPENED.
21 years ago	• YOSHIMI KUROISHI IS WORKING AS A BUTLER FOR THE KOGAMIS WHEN HE SUDDENLY MARRIES.
20 years ago	• THE KUROISHIS' ONLY CHILD MEGUMI (A SON) IS BORN. *goo goo ga ga*
17 years ago	• THE KOGAMIS' ONLY CHILD SUZUKA (A DAUGHTER) IS BORN. *Waaah!*
14 years ago	• THE KUROISHIS RECEIVE WORD THAT THE KOGAMIS HAVE DISAPPEARED DURING A TRIP TO RURAL CHINA. PAPA KUROISHI IS WORRIED.
12 years ago	• (THIS WAS FOUND OUT LATER...) MR. AND MRS. KOGAMI DIE OF A SUDDEN ILLNESS. ONLY SUZUKA SURVIVES.
Six months ago	• SUZUKA IS FOUND IN CHINA, HAVING BEEN RAISED BY ADOPTED PARENTS.
	• SUZUKA RETURNS TO JAPAN. (FOR THE FIRST TIME IN 14 YEARS.)
	• **THE EFFECTS OF THE CURSE ARE FIRST SEEN! MEGUMI IS STRONGLY INFLUENCED BY IT.**
A few months ago	• THANKS TO MEGUMI'S FRIEND SAGARA, MEGUMI AND SUZUKA'S RELATIONSHIP BECOMES CLOSER.
A short while ago	• THEIR RELATIONSHIP DEEPENS MORE AS HIRYU TAKATSUKASA, HEIR TO A GREAT FORTUNE, COMES BETWEEN THEM.
Present day	• IT STARTS ON THE NEXT PAGE.

CURSE

HOW RIDICULOUS!

FOR SUZUKA

STA——RE

HA...

AH!

Normal

...HUH?

Don't look at me like that!

IT HAS TO BE BECAUSE OF THE CURSE!

Soo funny.

YOU'RE TOTALLY IN LOVE WITH HER!!

Ha ha ha!

Ah ha ha!

I'M GOING HOME.

YOU HAVE TERRIBLE TIMING. TODAY IN BIOLOGY WE LEARNED ABOUT FUNGI.

Suzuka has that class too...

YOU'RE SO OBLIVIOUS TO EVERY-THING.

stare

SHALL I SEE YOU OUT, RICH LITTLE TAKATSU-KASA?

I'LL PASS.

I HAVE SHIBATA FOR THAT.

...Fine then.

Ha Ah ha ha ha ha ha ha ha ha!

I HOPE YOU DIE FROM LAUGH-ING.

GREAT... THE CURSE IS MAKING ME NOT CARE ABOUT HOW I LOOK IN FRONT OF OTHERS!

SHOCK

SHOCK

Urrrahhh...

I REALLY THOUGHT HARD ABOUT LETTING YOU HAVE SUZUKA.

Hmph.

clink

WELL ...

WHEN HE MADE US TEA.

While you were lost in ecstasy

?

HUH? A LETTER? WHEN DID HE DO THAT?

OH, WAIT. BEFORE I FORGET... YOUR DAD GAVE THIS TO ME.

much much

I GUESS I'LL GO HOME TOO.

HE SEEMED LIKE HE WAS IN A HURRY AND DIDN'T SAY MUCH.

...?!

See you, lovebirds! ♡

FRENZY

112

I have a certain set of concepts for the *Captive Hearts* illustrations!

They're a little random, ♦ But I'll write them anyway. Here they are!!

(1) Megumi and Suzuka's Bodies must be connected in some way.
(2) CHAINS. It's CAPTIVE Hearts, after all.
(3) SHACKLES. It's CAPTIVE Hearts, after all.
(4) A CAGE, JAIL CELL OR IRON BARS. It's CAPTIVE Hearts, after all.
(5) RIBBONS in place of ropes. It's CAPTIVE Hearts, after all.
(6) Formal(ish) clothing.
(7) I aim for: racy, passionate, fairy-tale-like, Body-guard-ish (and for some reason mafia-themed) illustrations.

I usually pick at least two out of these seven and make an illustration of it. I also include that criteria for the manga covers!

124

...I CAN'T FORGIVE THIS "SERVANT'S CURSE" BECAUSE IT DOES THE SAME THING!!

SO UNTIL THE CURSE IS BROKEN...

...I WON'T AGREE TO THIS!

IT'S UNFORGIVEABLE!

Y-YOU'RE RIGHT!

whom?

...!

Right now?!

WE HAVE TO GO TO HUANG-SAN!

WE HAVE TO DO IT NOW!

MEGUMI!

SOMEONE WITH QUITE AN UNUSUAL CURSE HAS COME...

Come here, come here.

MY, MY...

WE'VE COME TO ASK YOUR ADVICE.

ARE YOU HUANG-SAN?

In Chinese.

...?

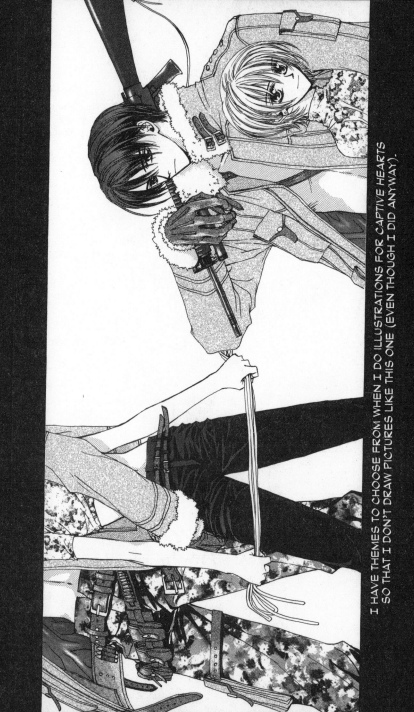

I HAVE THEMES TO CHOOSE FROM FOR WHEN I DO ILLUSTRATIONS FOR *CAPTIVE HEARTS* SO THAT I DON'T DRAW PICTURES LIKE THIS ONE (EVEN THOUGH I DID ANYWAY).

Captive Hearts

141

SLAVE TRADER BOSSES FROM ALL OVER ASIA ARE NOW IN CUSTODY IN THIS COUNTRY.

ARJUNA AND SUZUKA WERE KIDNAPPED BY THIS RING WHEN THEY WERE YOUNG...

IF THEY CAN IDENTIFY THEM, THE CRIMINALS WILL BE ARRESTED.

YOU'RE SO COLD-HEARTED.

IT'S BUSI-NESS.

FROM SUZUKA'S REAC-TION... ...I CAN TELL SHE HASN'T REMEM-BERED EVERY-THING.

click

DO YOU THINK SHE CAN HELP US WITHIN FOUR DAYS, ARJ?

GROOM

BLUBBERING

But I AM sad that Megu-chan hates me, after alllll!!

WAAAAAAAAAH!

WAAAAAAAH!

yes, yes, I know

col-lapse

THE REASON I'M HERE... IS BECAUSE OF HIM.

ALL I REMEMBER ABOUT ARJ...

...IS THAT HE GAVE ME SO MUCH COURAGE.

HE'S THE ONE WHO SAVED ME FROM MY TERRIFYING PRISON.

...AND I WAS SO OVERWHELMED THAT I BLANKED OUT...

Ah ha ha...

I SUDDENLY REMEMBERED THAT...

lean

I'M SORRY.

148

NOW'S NOT THE TIME FOR ME TO BE JEALOUS.

I HAVE TO PROTECT YOU...

squeeze

...FROM ALL THE BAD THINGS, PAST AND PRESENT...

I'LL TRY MY BEST TO REMEMBER THE THINGS I FORGOT.

THANK YOU, MEGUMI...

SHOCK

...

I HAVE TO... ...HELP YOUR MOTHER.

SO THEY CAN CATCH THE CRIMINALS.

I MUST PROTECT YOU!

Noo!! You don't have to!!

BUT...

It's not good for you to remember those horrible things!

IS IT ALL RIGHT IF I SERVE BY YOUR SIDE AGAIN THEN?

...

YES, STAY BY ME!

YES! YOU HAVE MY FULL DEVOTION!

HUH?

PRINCESS...

YOU CAN'T DO SOMETHING LIKE THAT!

I DON'T CARE IF YOU'RE RUDE!

What does that even mean?

Just now, I've been reborn as a "slave of love"!

AND YOU SORT OF REMEMBER HOW ARJ'S QUICK THINKING HELPED YOU ESCAPE FROM YOUR CAPTORS?

YES...

I SEE... SO YOU ONLY HAVE A VAGUE MEMORY OF WHEN YOUR PARENTS DIED AND WHEN YOUR ADOPTIVE PARENTS TOOK YOU IN...

5

The Editor Legend!

My editor "T-san" is beautiful and looks great in Chinese dresses. She always gives me great advice, so I have a lot of confidence in her.

However...

She has a very strange talent. This frequently happened while I was still working at a bookstore. My shift there would end late, and I'd get home about an hour and a half later than usual. I'd open the front door, and as soon as I'd step in...

RINNNNNG

She'd always call at that exact moment! It happened all the time. (Maybe there are hidden cameras in my apartment?!)

HM?

I KNOW IT'S HARD, BUT I NEED YOU TO.

BUT YOU HAVE TO REMEMBER MORE ABOUT WHEN YOU WERE KID-NAPPED...

BY THE WAY, MEGU-CHAN.

I'LL TRY ...!

I... ...!

WHY, SERVING MISTRESS HER TEA, OF COURSE.

ROOOOAR

STUCK CLOSELY

WHAT THE HECK ARE YOU DOING?

...YOUR LOVE SLAVE, SWEAR TO PROTECT YOU!

IF THAT EVIL WOMAN TRIES TO GET VIOLENT, I, MEGUMI...

Here you go...

...Prin-cess! ♡

...

SNAP

155

I'M FINE!

I'M NOT A CRYBABY LIKE I USED TO BE!

...SAVE THOSE CHILDREN!

I WANT TO HELP KEITO-SAN...

YOU'VE GOTTEN STRONGER...

FOUR DAYS LEFT UNTIL THE DEADLINE...

158

SUZUKA...

THREE DAYS UNTIL THE DEADLINE...

161

...

THEY RAN AWAY.

IT'S FINE.

THAT MIGHT BE WHAT SHE NEEDS.

LET'S GO SOMEWHERE WHERE YOU CAN FORGET EVERYTHING AND SLEEP.

JUST TO REST.

166

168

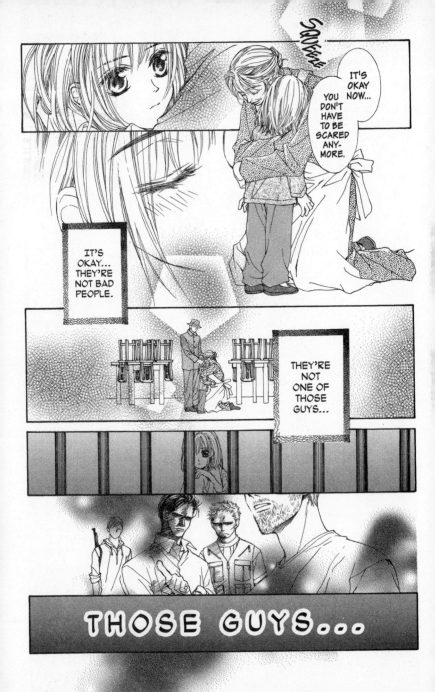

SHIVER

THE ONES WITH SUCH COLD EYES...

...

whoosh

AN UNFA-MILIAR CEILING....

...?

GOOD MORNING.

OH

ARE YOU SURPRISED TO WAKE UP IN A STRANGE PLACE?

WE'RE AT A HOTEL.

A hotel!?

UH... MEGUMI...?

UHH...

YEAH... I SLEPT REALLY WELL...

THANKS...

SO YOU PROBABLY DON'T REMEMBER...

Of course...

YOU WERE ALREADY SOUND ASLEEP WHEN I BROUGHT YOU HERE LAST NIGHT.

174

6

A lot has happened between the first and second volumes.

① For the first time in my career, one of my comics (Captive Hearts) had a second printing!! (Volume 1)

② I got to speak with other artists from Hana to Yume. (I was so happy to meet them for the first time!) ♡♡

③ The story about me meeting them was published in Haku-sensha's free news-letter...unfortunately with pictures of me laughing stupidly, being nervous, and acting cool! (So embar-rassing!) ♪♪

④ I won the "Athena" award.

⑤ Had pages in color for the first time...

⑥ Got the cover of LaLa magazine for the first time...

⑦ Captive Hearts was picked up for serialization again! (My fourth "new" published work! Awesome!)

⑧ I got tons of letters! ♡♡♡

● ● ●

Lots of great things happened... I'm really grateful. I'll keep do-ing my best! (Am I just boasting?!) ♪♪♪
See you! ♡

YOU SPOIL ME TOO MUCH, MEGUMI.

LET'S HURRY AND END THIS, OKAY?

... HEY.

I THINK SHE'S YELLING FOR YOU...

Yaa~y! Yaa~ry! Thank you!! You're the best, ya soon! Suzuka-chan!

throb

Ahh!

188

DID I MAKE HER CRY?!

sizzle

WHY IS SHE CRYING SO LOUDLY...?

....!

ゴゴゴゴ...!

THIS IS ALL I CAN DO FOR HER RIGHT NOW...

...SO I NEED TO MAKE HER EAT.

SUZUKA HASN'T HAD MUCH OF AN APPETITE LATELY...

sizzle

...

SHE'S...

...USUALLY SUCH A CRYBABY...

...LIKE ARJ CAN. HE EXPERIENCED THOSE HORRIBLE THINGS WITH HER...

I CAN'T UNDERSTAND WHAT SHE'S GOING THROUGH...

sizzle

sizzzzle

...

BUT WHY HASN'T SHE CRIED YET?

SHE WAS PROBABLY SO SCARED...

189

YOU'RE GOING HOME ALREADY?

YEAH... MY HOME-STAY HERE IS ALMOST OVER.

I skipped school a lot though...

LET'S KEEP IN TOUCH, OKAY?

OKAY.

AFTER THAT, SUZUKA DIDN'T TELL ME ANY-THING ELSE ABOUT THE INCIDENT.

WELL, UNTIL I SEE YOU AGAIN...

OKAY...

TAKE CARE...

ARJ...!

Prompt answer

IT'S NOT A VERY INTER-ESTING STORY.

THAT'S WHAT SHE SAID NONCHA-LANTLY...

ARJ...

VROOOOM

194

BECAUSE I WANT YOUR PRESENT, MEGUMI!

SO I HAVE TO MAKE SURE THE HOLES DON'T CLOSE!

HER EXISTENCE...

...BINDS ME TO HER...

...AND WON'T LET GO...

klak klak klak klak klak klak klak

I WAS AVOIDING YOU BECAUSE I WAS AFRAID OF THIS!

↑ True motive

I TOLD YOU, IT'S NOT MY FAULT!

ARRGH!!!

Give me back my normal Megu-cha~~~n!!!

On vacation

CAN WE PLEASE JUST HAVE A NORMAL GAME?

In order for Princess to win, I, Megumi Kuroishi (her love slave), will do absolutely anythijijing!!

PRIN-CESS!! FIGHT!

RUMBLE

Captive Hearts 2 / The End

Captive Hearts

Comic Strip Theater

I think
my
mommy
and
daddy...

...are
weirdos...

Kuroishi-san's Family Situation

... MEGUMI TURNED INTO THIS KIND OF PERSON.

SUZUKA'S EARS ARE SO CUTE...

AW...

!!!

The end.

THIS IS THE END OF VOLUME 2.

DID IT MAKE YOUR HEART RACE?

I'M ALREADY THINKING OF THE NEXT STORY...

...SO I'LL BE WORKING HARD ON VOLUME 3! ♡

Thanks for reading!

May 2000   Matsuri Hino

Kuroishi-san's Family Situation / The End

Captivated by the story but confused by some of the terms? Here are some cultural notes to help you out!

HONORIFICS

Chan – an informal version of *san* used to address children and females.

Kun – an informal honorific used primarily for males; it can be used by people of more senior status addressing those junior to them or by anyone in addressing male children.

San – the most common honorific title; it is used to address people outside one's immediate family and close circle of friends.

Sama – the formal version of *san*; this honorific title is used primarily in addressing persons much higher in rank than oneself.

NOTES

Page 4, panel 1 – **Muromachi Period**
A period of Japanese history that ran from approximately 1336 to 1573. It ended when the last shogun, Ashikaga Yoshiaki, was driven out of the capital, Kyoto, by Oda Nobunaga.

Page 4, panel 6 – **Ni Hao**
Ni hao means "hello" in Mandarin Chinese and is written 你好.

Page 79, panel 4 – **Xie Xie**
Xie xie means "thank you" in Mandarin Chinese and is written 謝謝.

Page 87, panel 5 – **Kanji**
Chinese characters that are used in the modern Japanese writing system.

Page 104, panel 1 – **Edo Period**
Also known as the Tokugawa Period, this era ran from 1603 to 1868.

Page 181, panel 6 – **Hana to Yume**
A Japanese *shojo manga* (girls' comics) magazine published by Hakusensha. The name translates to "Flowers and Dreams."

MATSURI HINO burst onto the manga scene with her title
Kono Yume ga Sametara (When This Dream Is Over), which was published
in *LaLa DX* magazine. Hino was a manga artist a mere nine months after
she decided to become one.

With the success of her popular series *Captive Hearts* and *MeruPuri*, Hino
has established herself as a major player in the world of shojo manga.
Vampire Knight is currently serialized in *LaLa* and *Shojo Beat* magazines.

Hino enjoys creative activities and has commented that she would
have been either an architect or an apprentice to traditional
Japanese craft masters if she had not become a manga artist.

Captive Hearts
Vol. 2

The Shojo Beat Manga Edition

STORY & ART BY
MATSURI HINO

Translation & Adaptation/Andria Cheng
Touch-up Art & Lettering/Sabrina Heep
Design/Amy Martin
Editor/Amy Yu

Editor in Chief, Books/Alvin Lu
Editor in Chief, Magazines/Marc Weidenbaum
VP, Publishing Licensing/Rika Inouye
VP, Sales & Product Marketing/Gonzalo Ferreyra
VP, Creative/Linda Espinosa
Publisher/Hyoe Narita

Toraware no Minoue by Matsuri Hino
© Matsuri Hino 1999
All rights reserved.
First published in Japan in 2000 by HAKUSENSHA, Inc., Tokyo.
English language translation rights arranged with Hakusensha, Inc., Tokyo.
The stories, characters and incidents mentioned in this publication are entirely fictional.

Printed in Canada

Published by VIZ Media, LLC
P.O. Box 77010
San Francisco, CA 94107

Shojo Beat Manga Edition
10 9 8 7 6 5 4 3 2 1
First printing, January 2009

S·A
Special A
by Maki Minami

Manga series on sale now

Only $8.99

Her whole life, Hikari Hanazono has been consumed with the desire to win against her school rival, Kei Takishima—at anything. He always comes out on top no matter what he does, and Hikari is determined to do whatever it takes to beat him!